Vol.2

THE BEST OF

FLOWER

MANDALA COLORING BOOKS FOR ADULTS

COLOR TEST PAGE

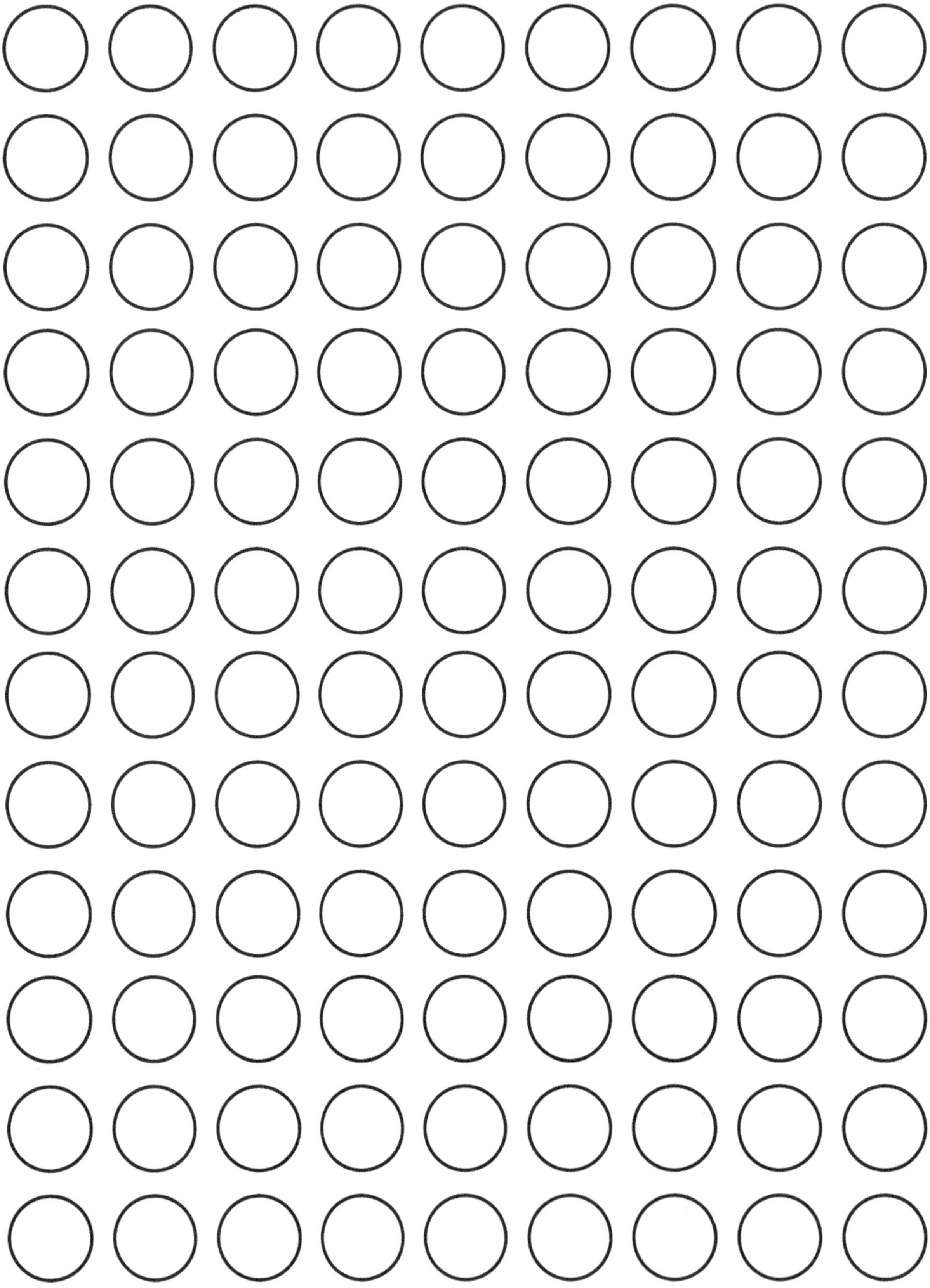

COLOR TEST PAGE

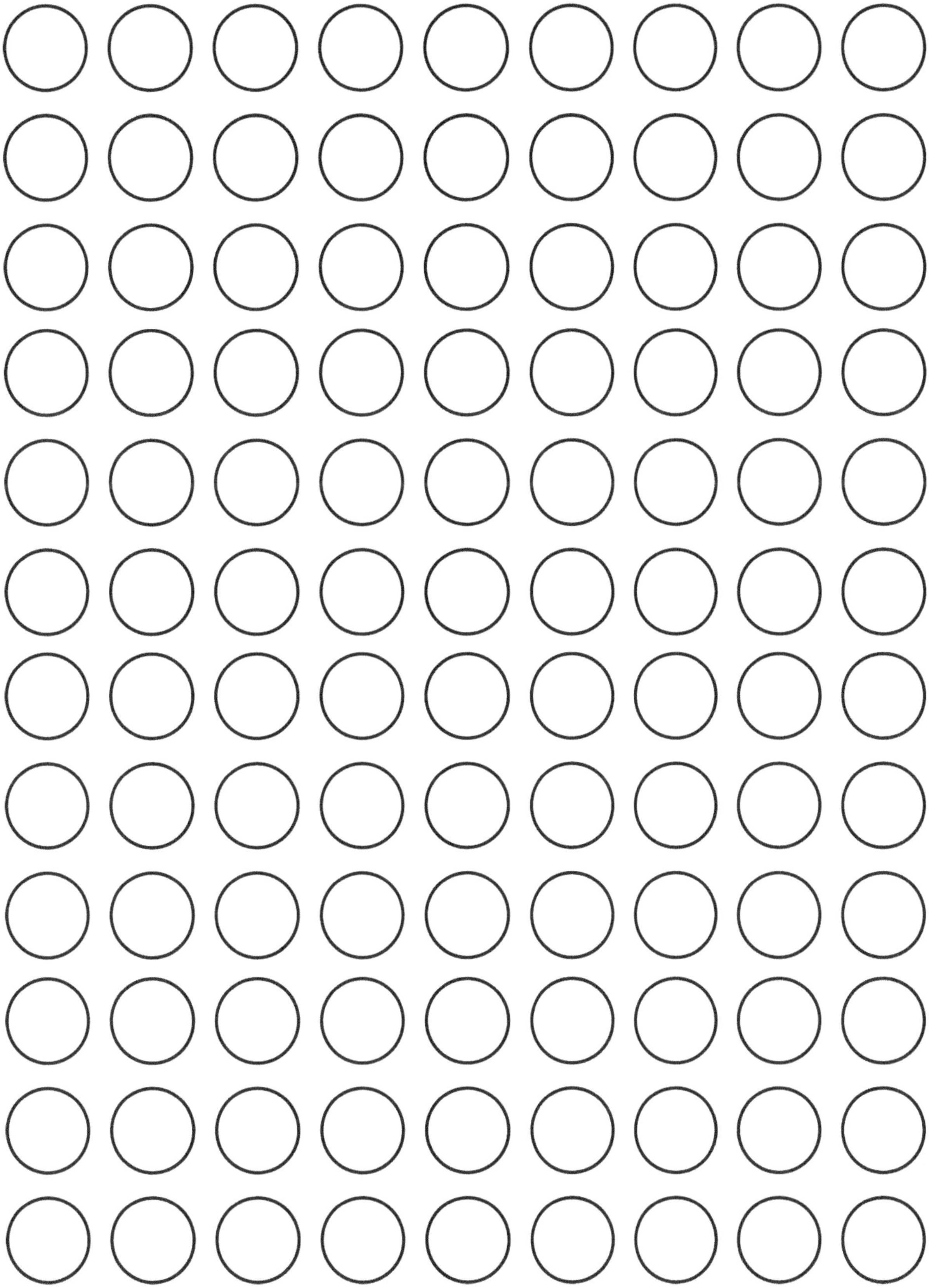

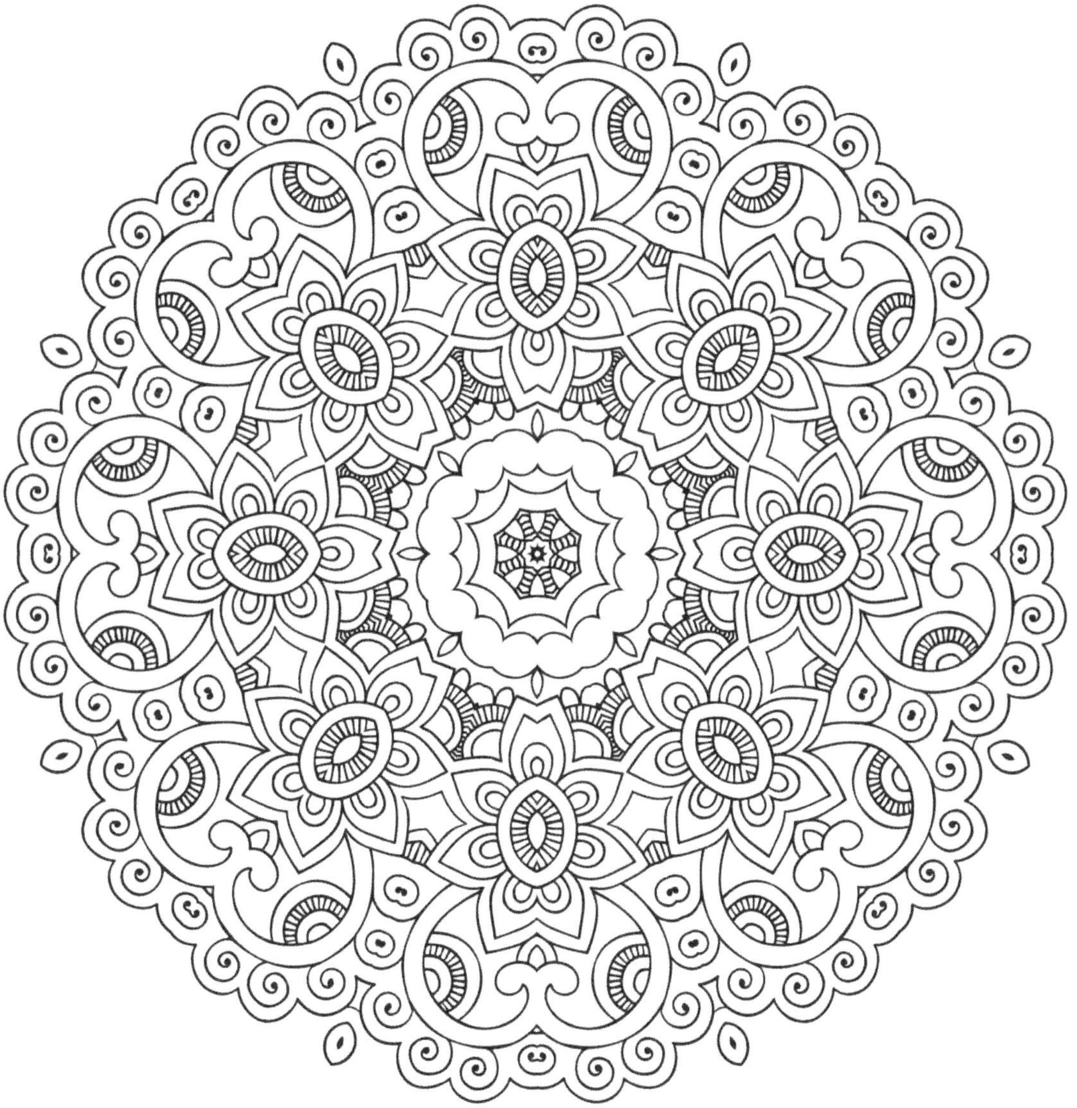

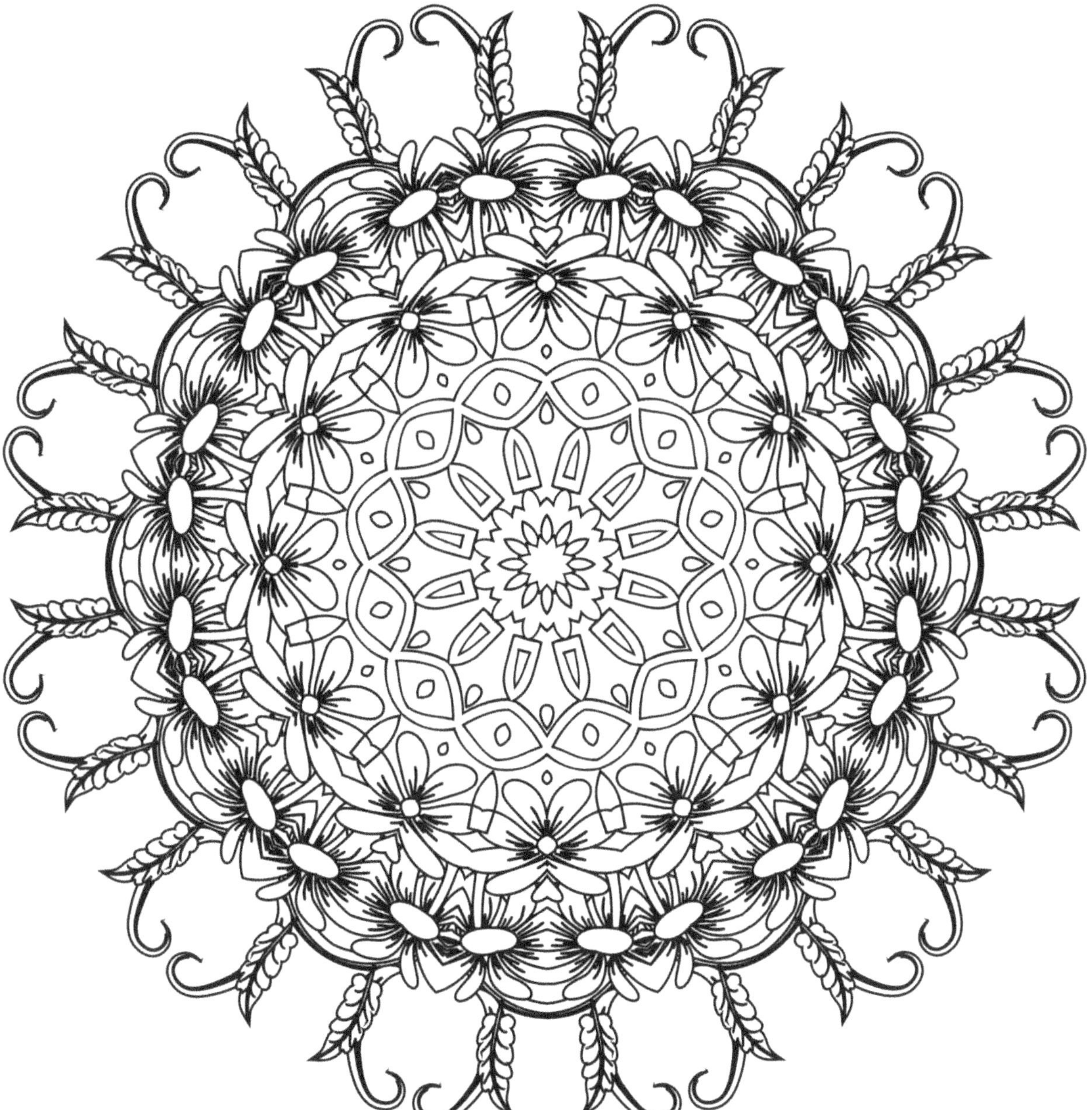

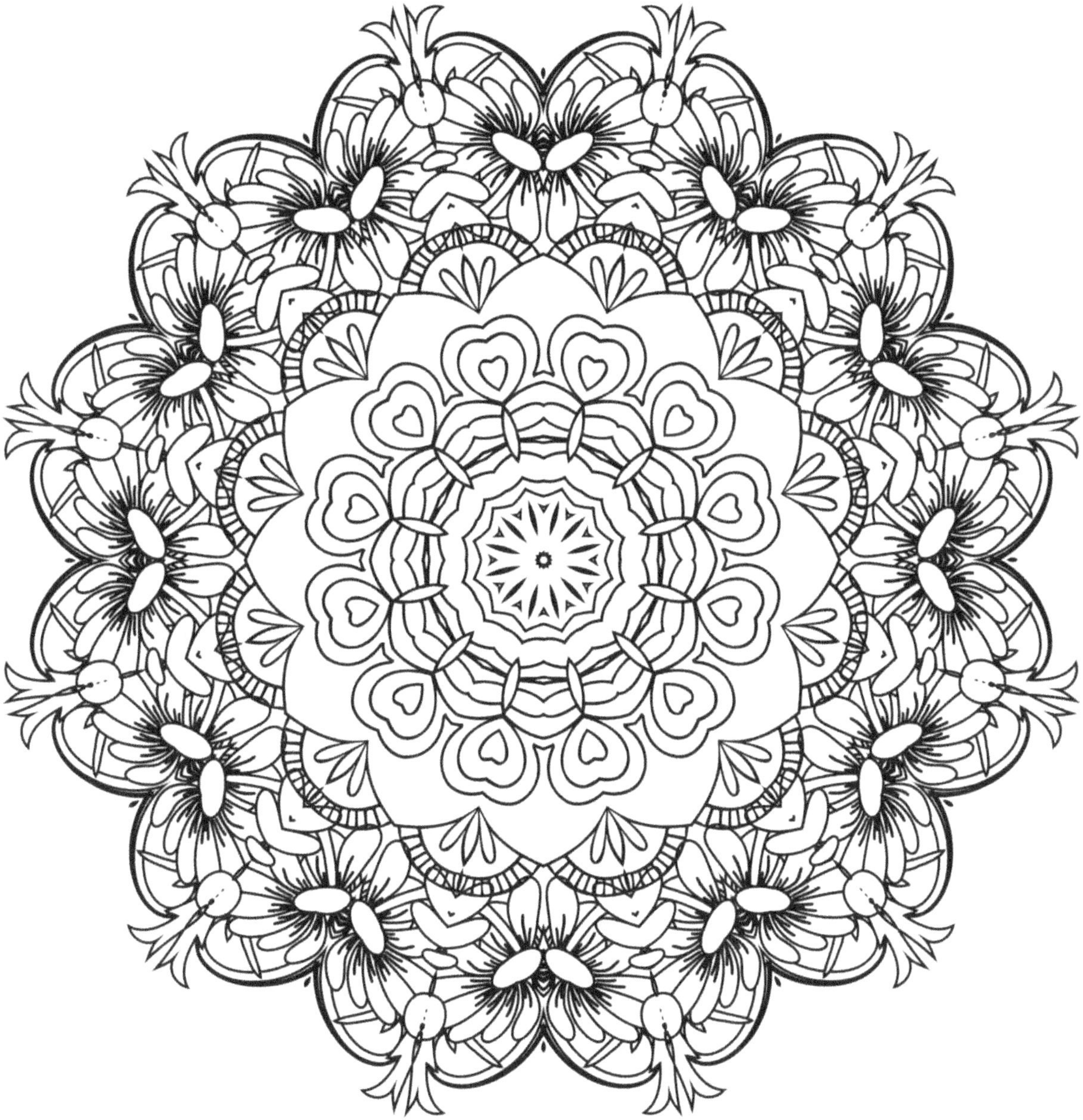

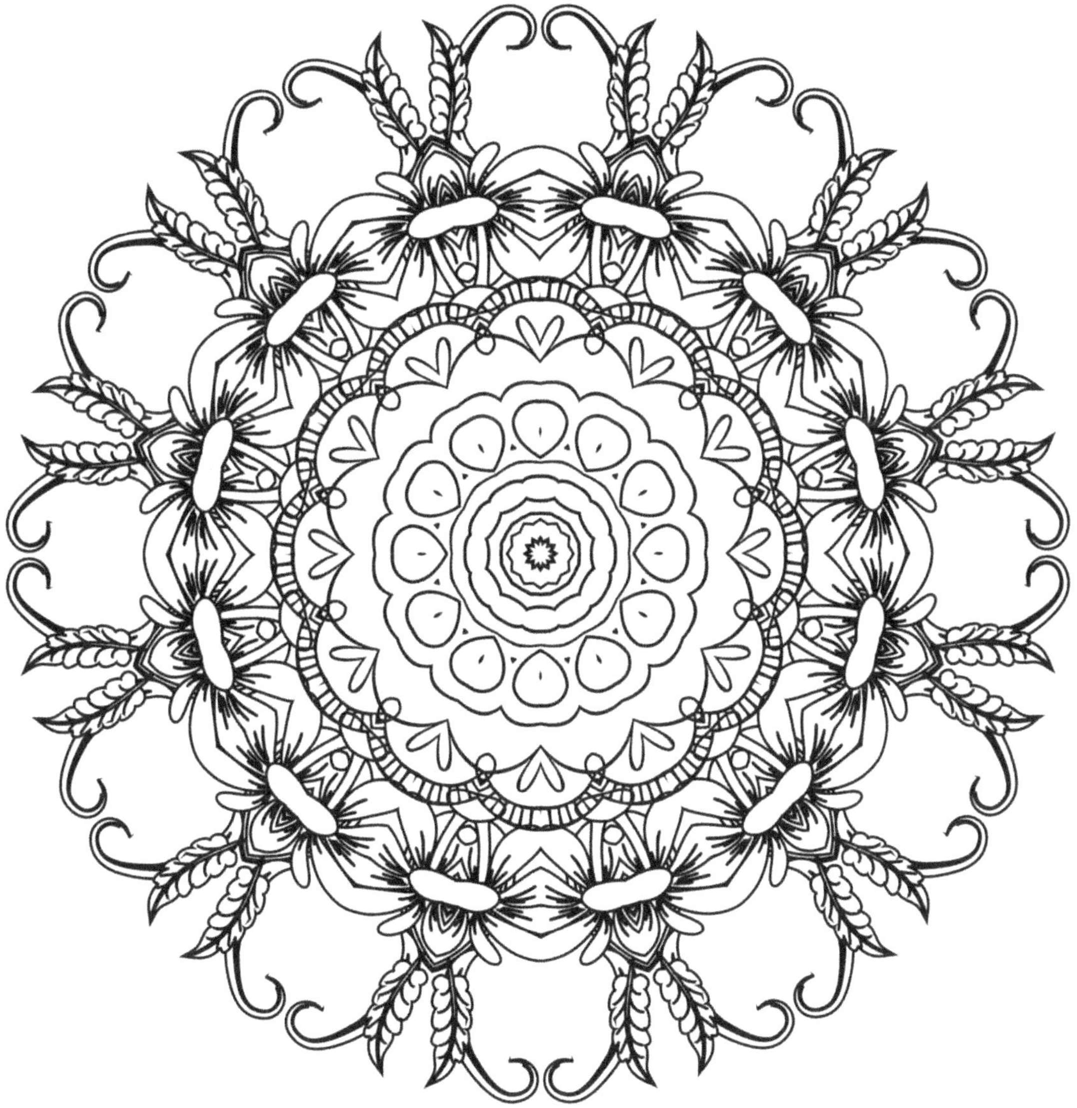

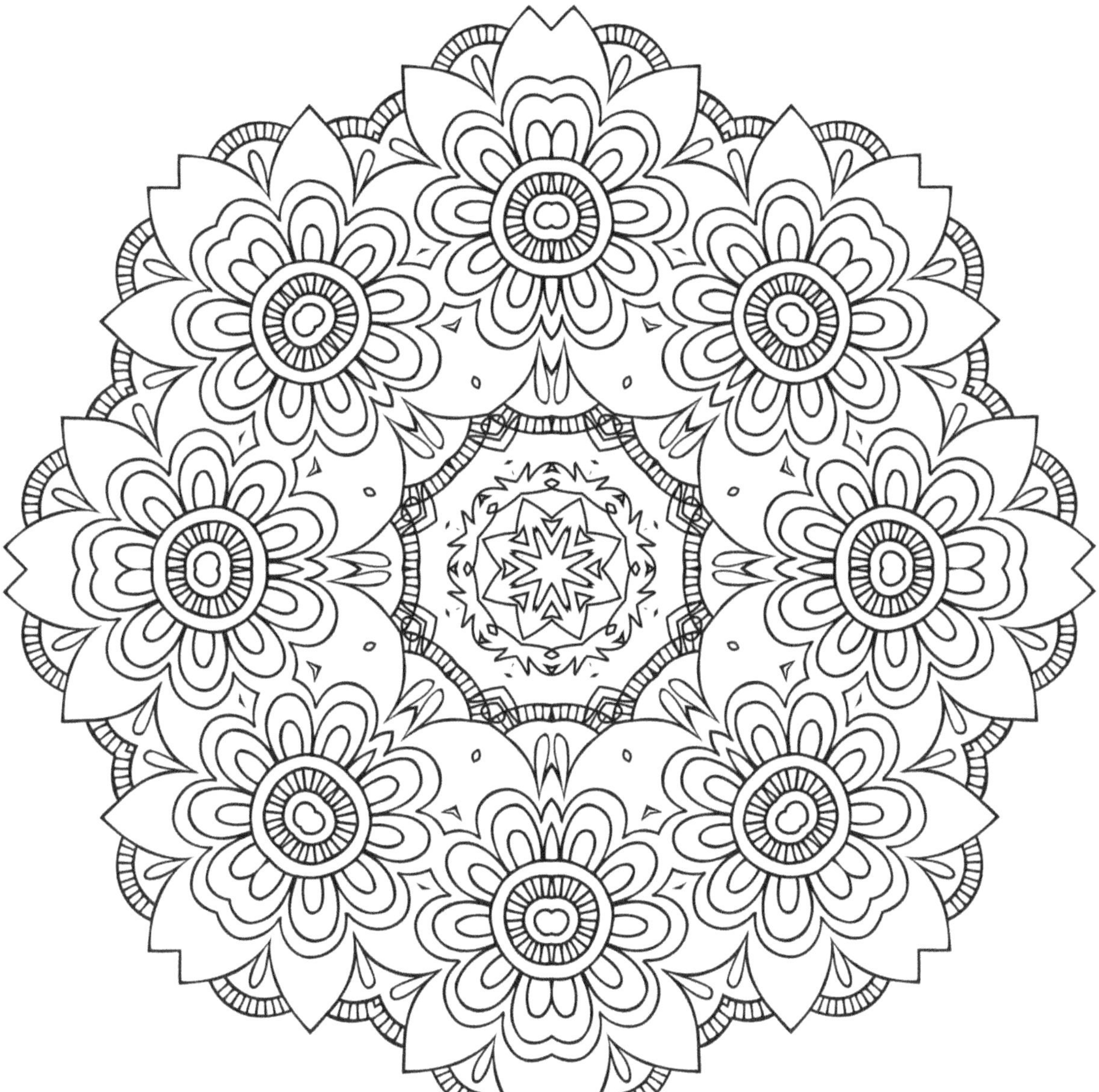

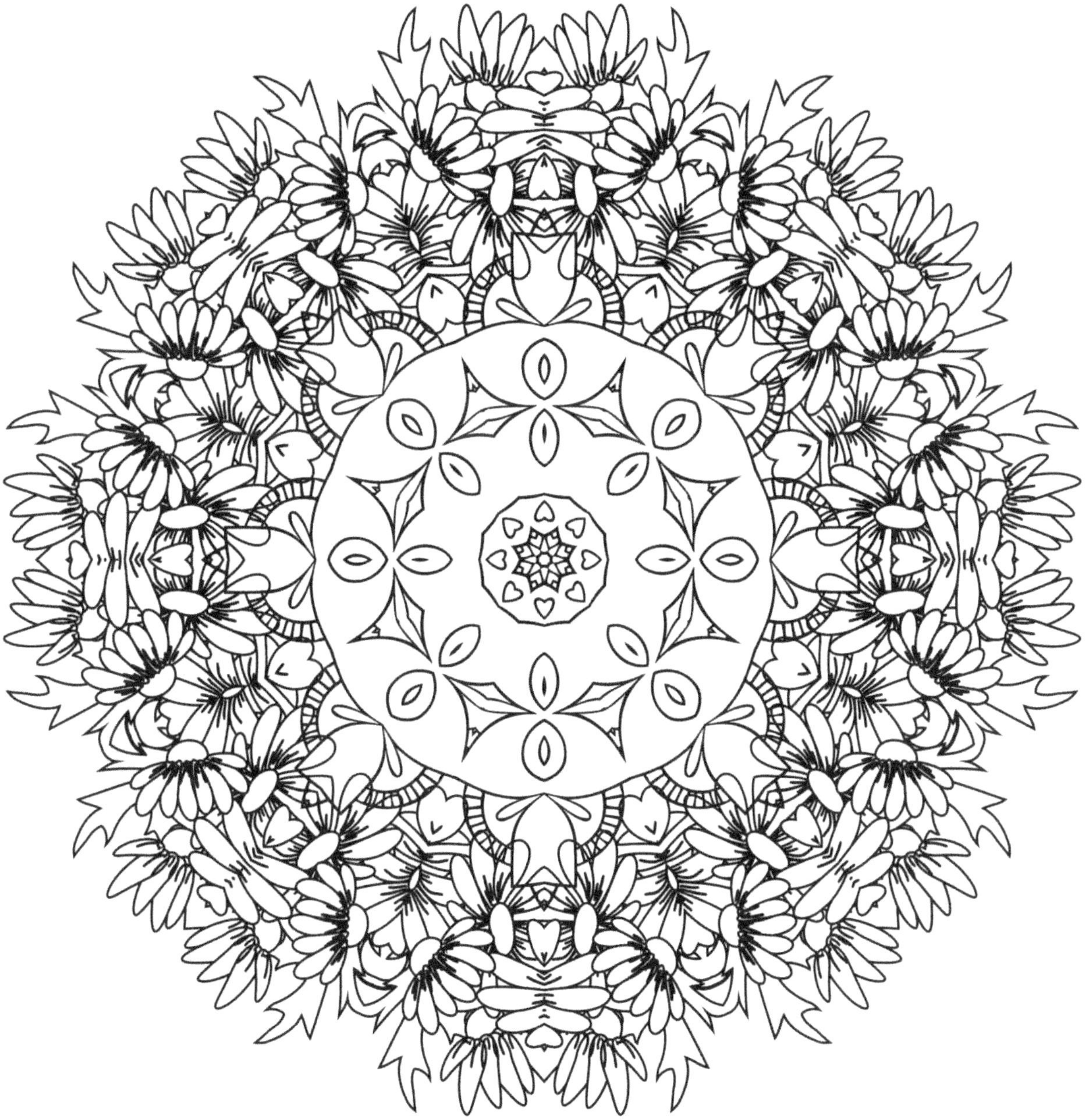

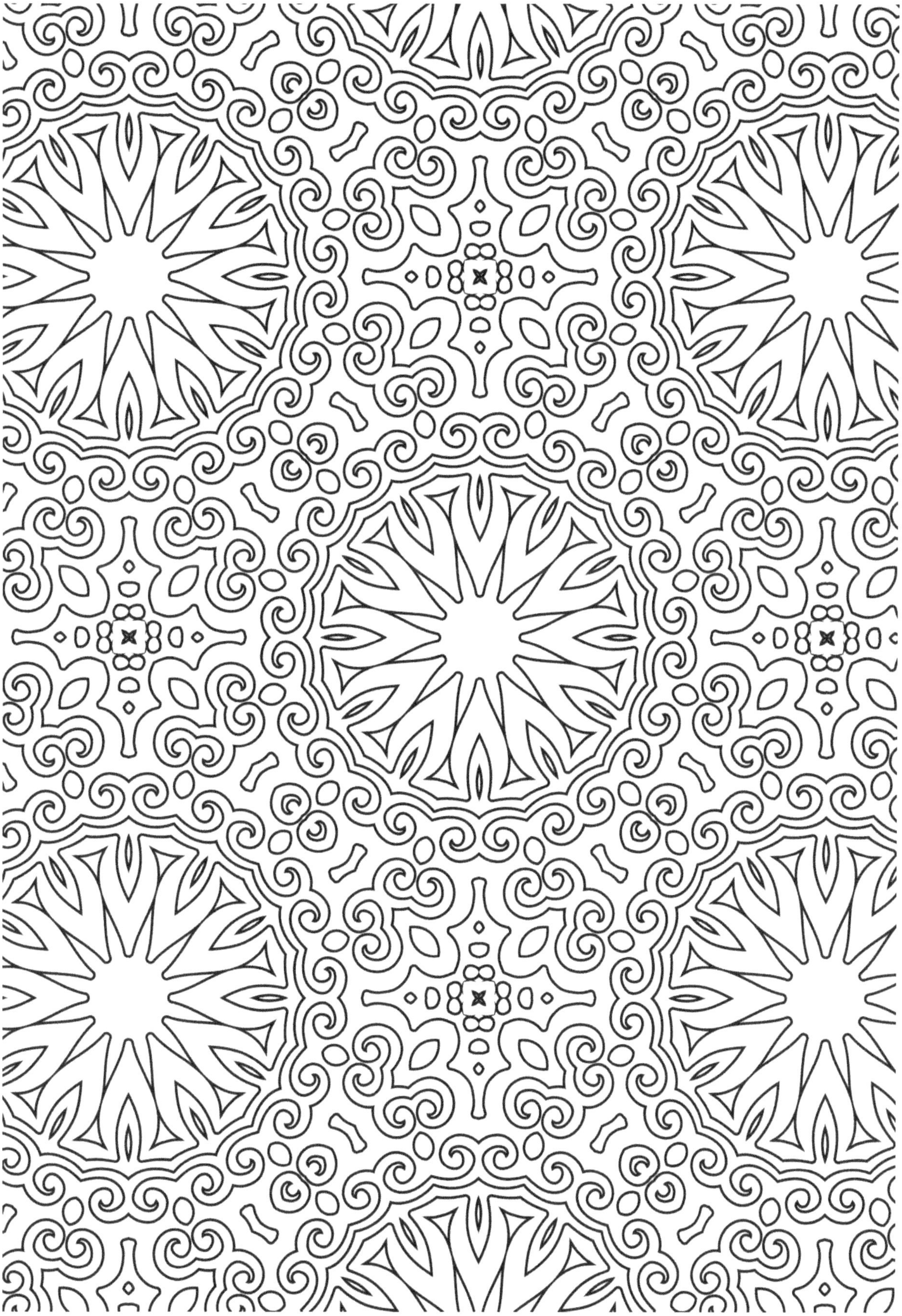

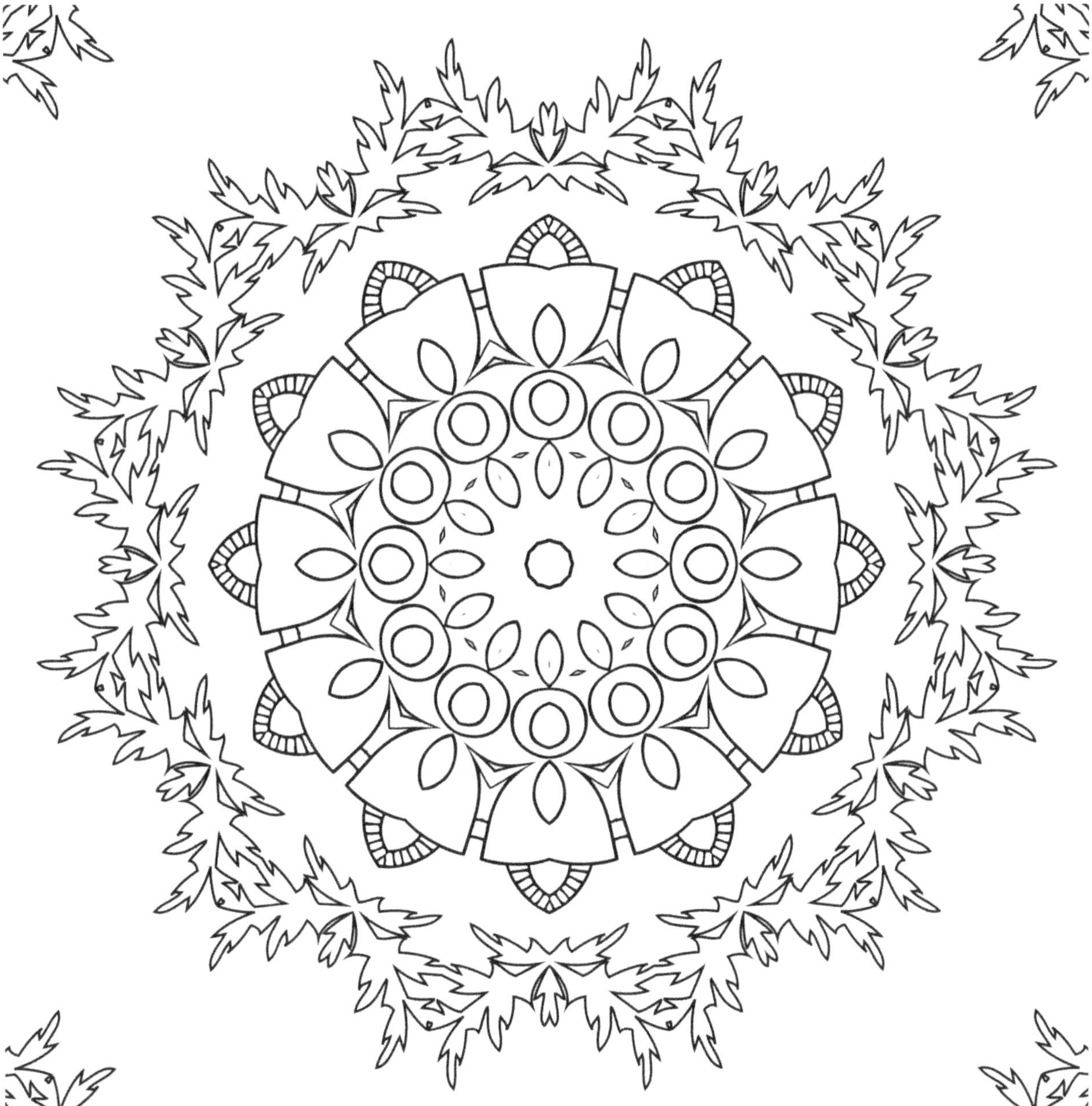

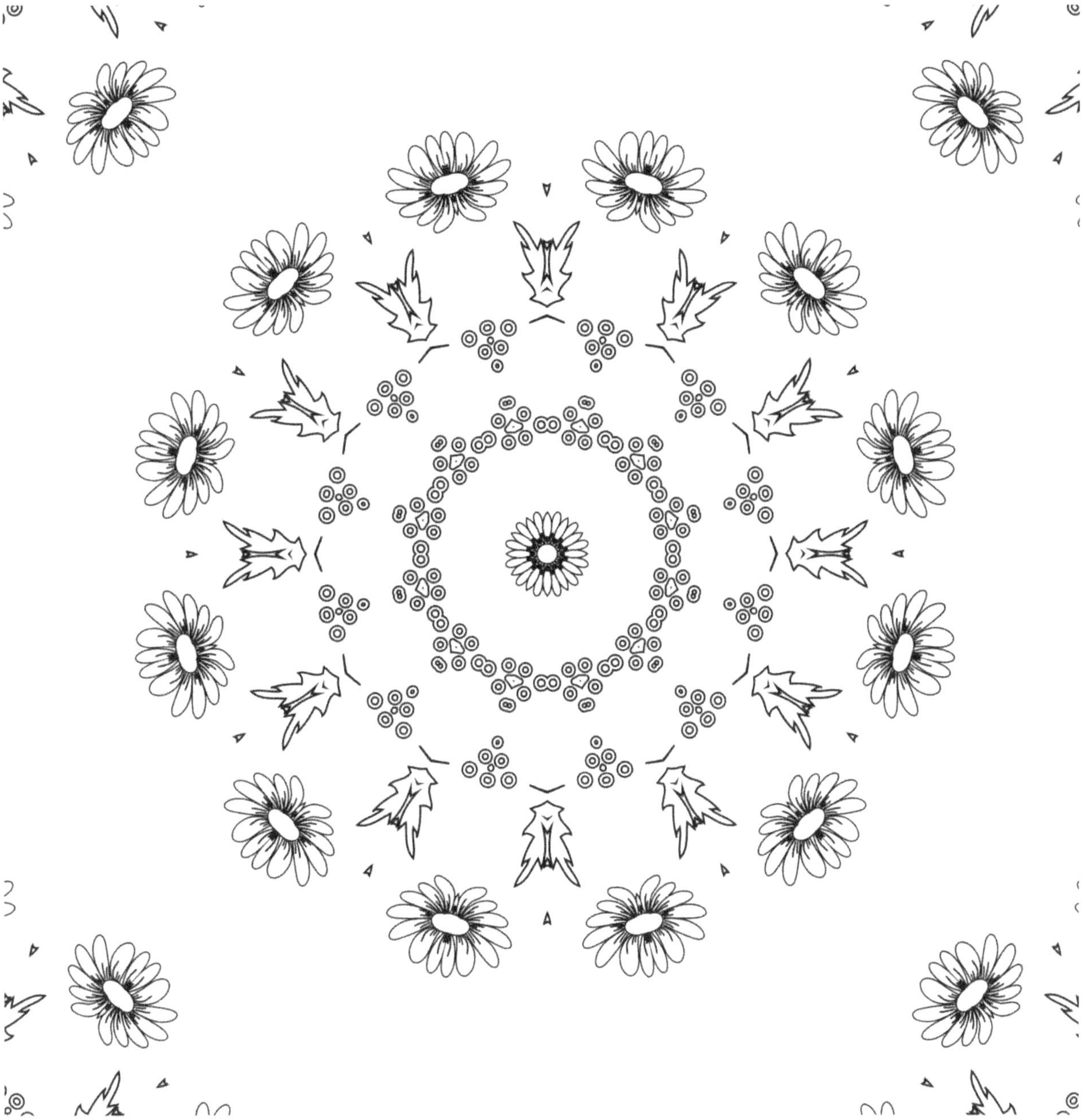

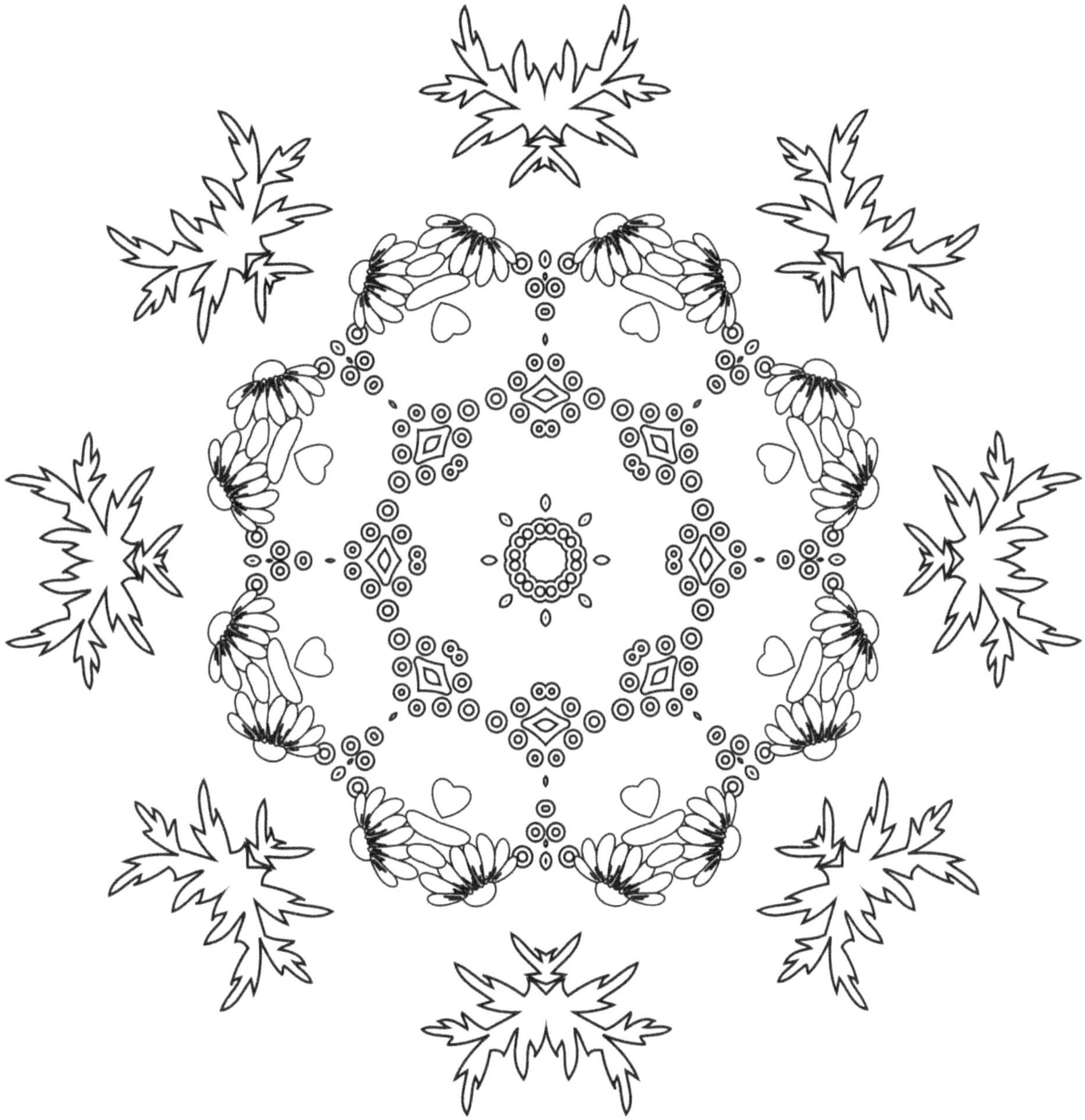

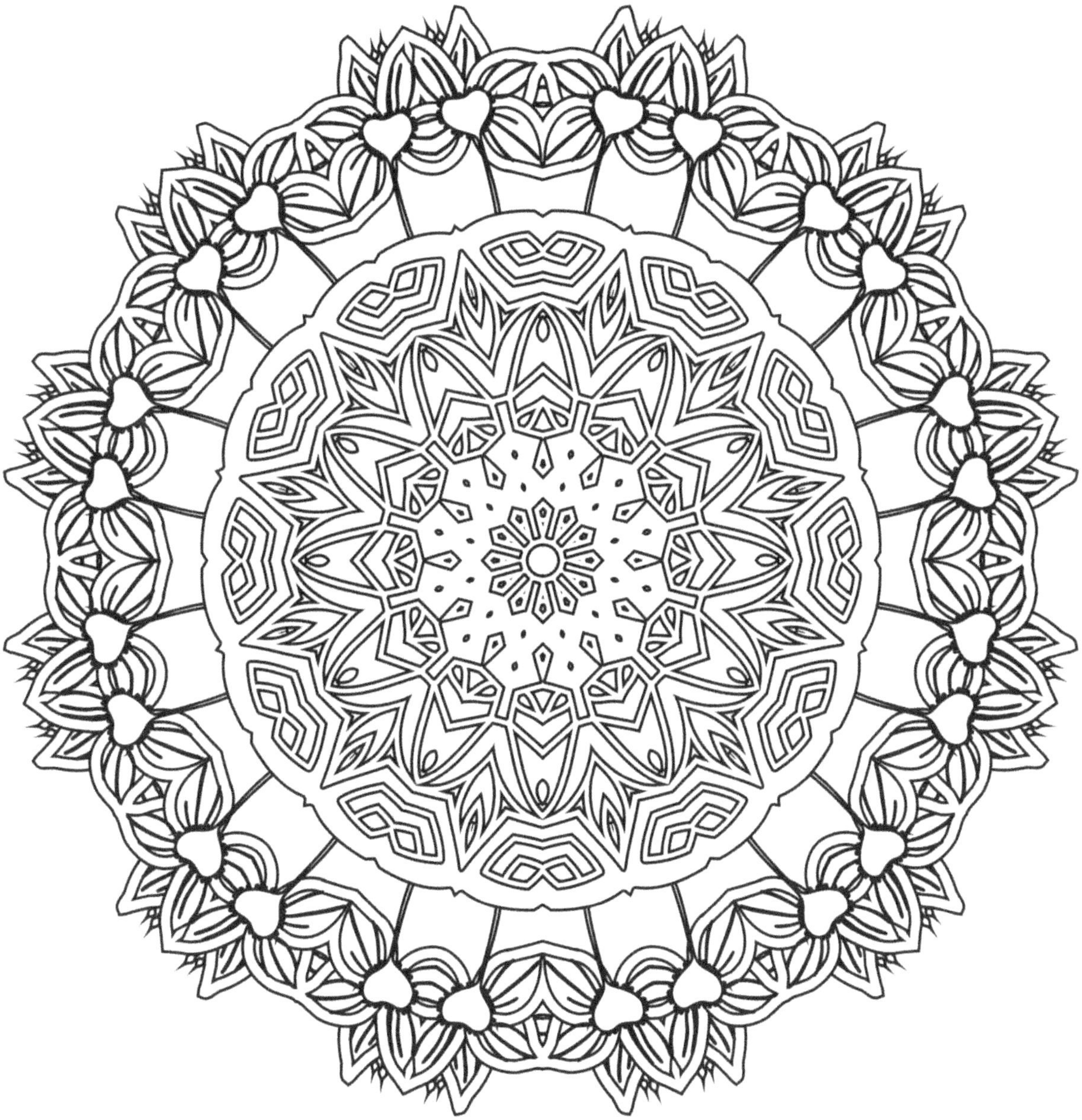

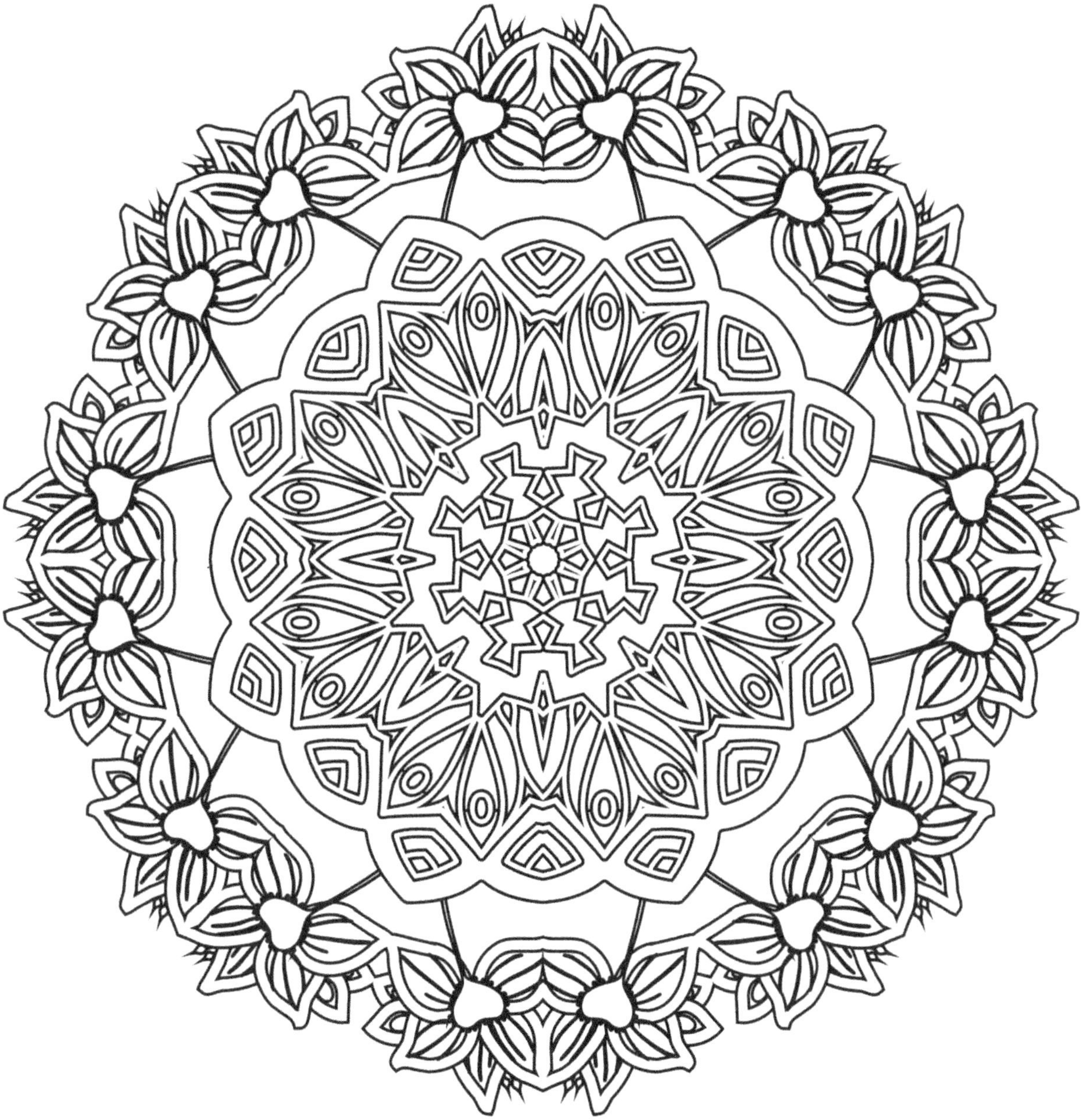

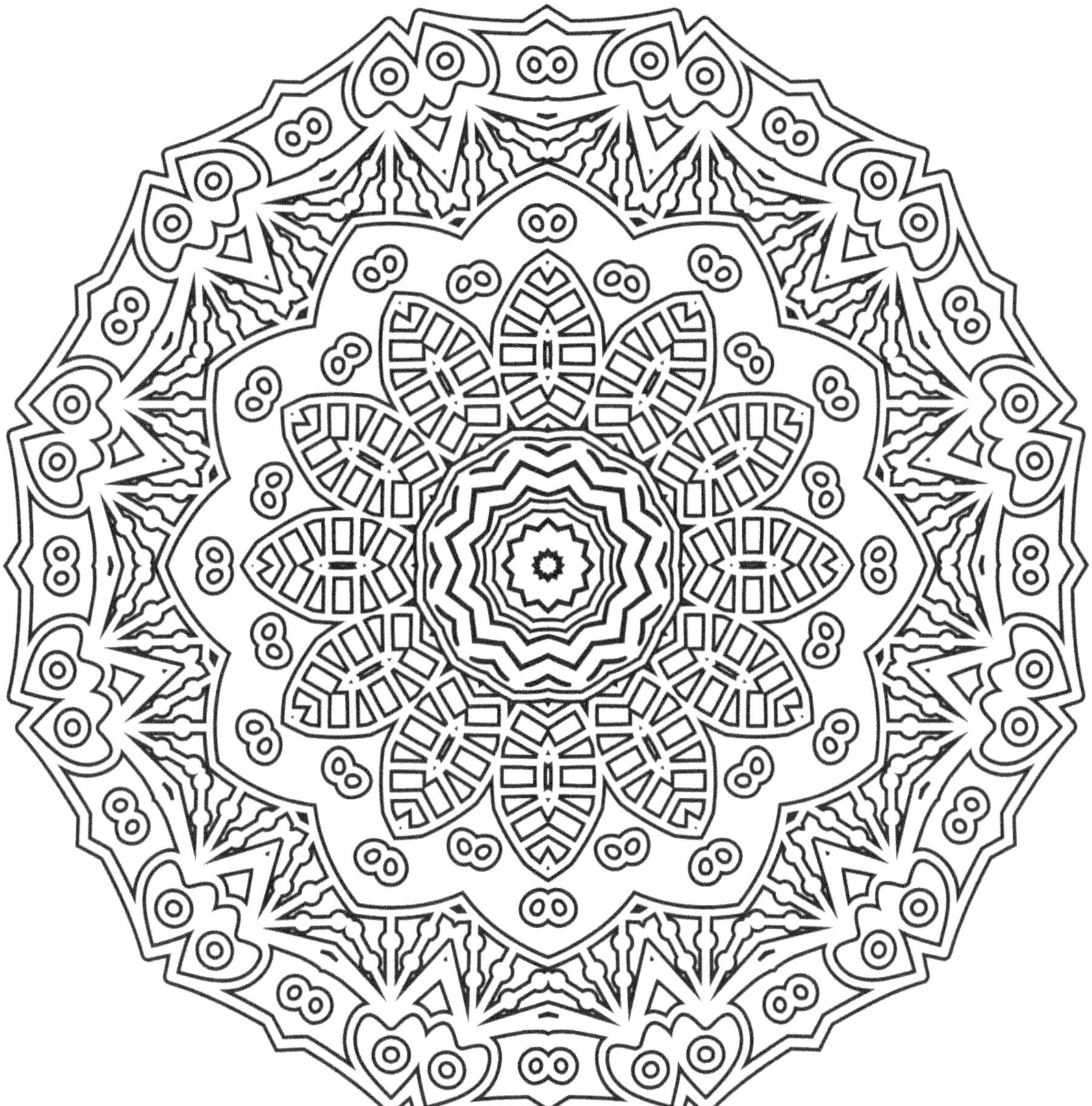

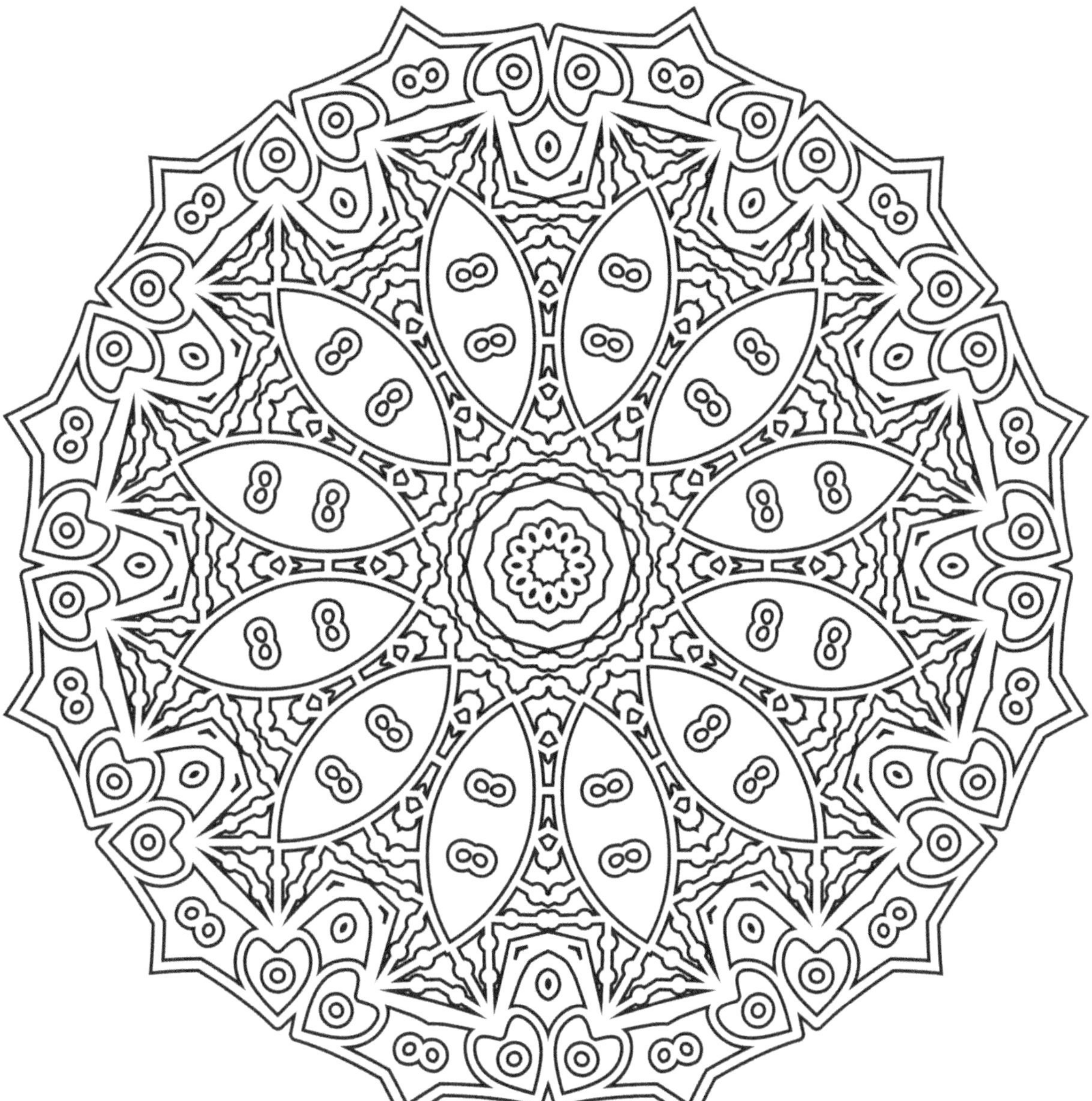

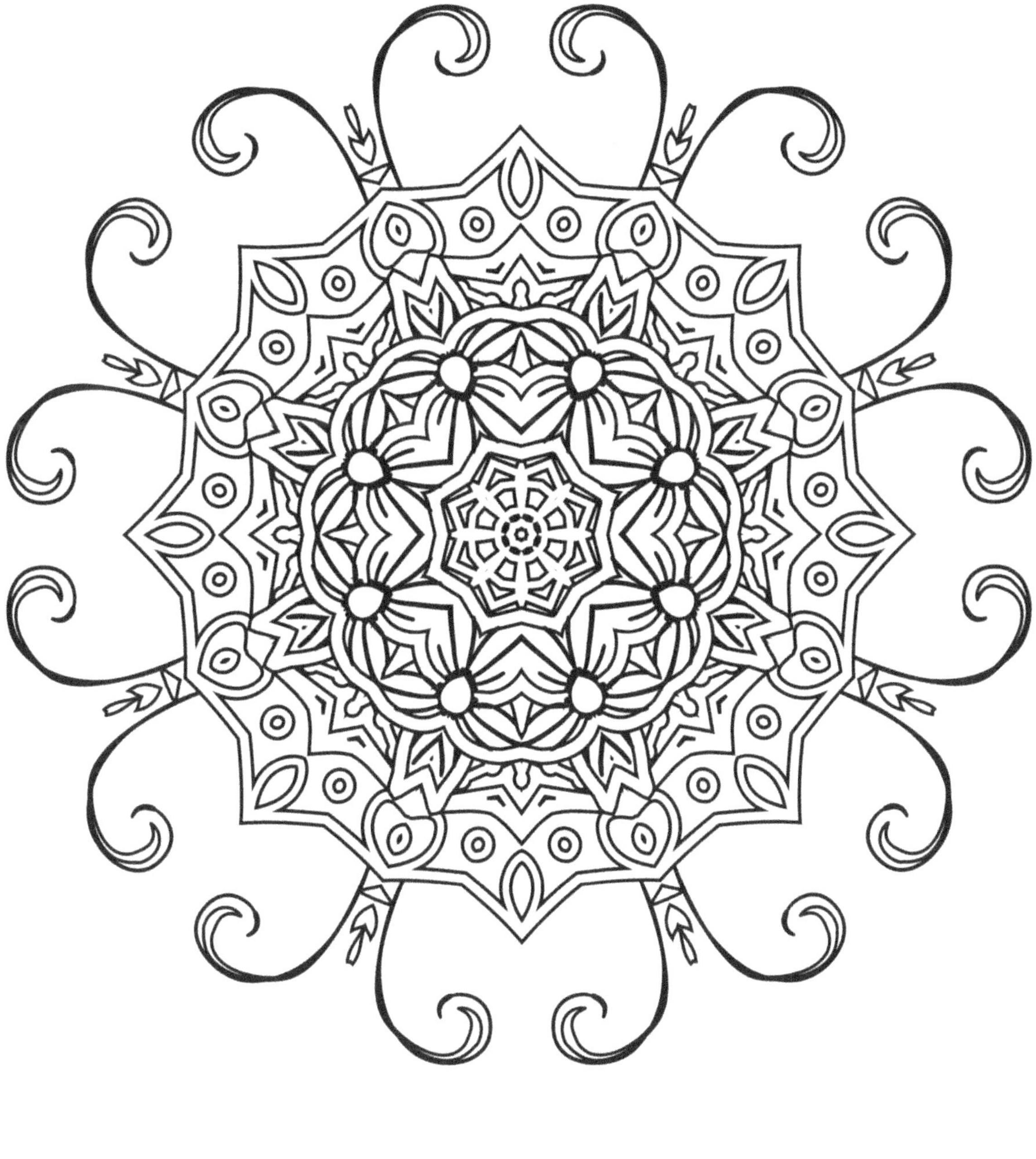

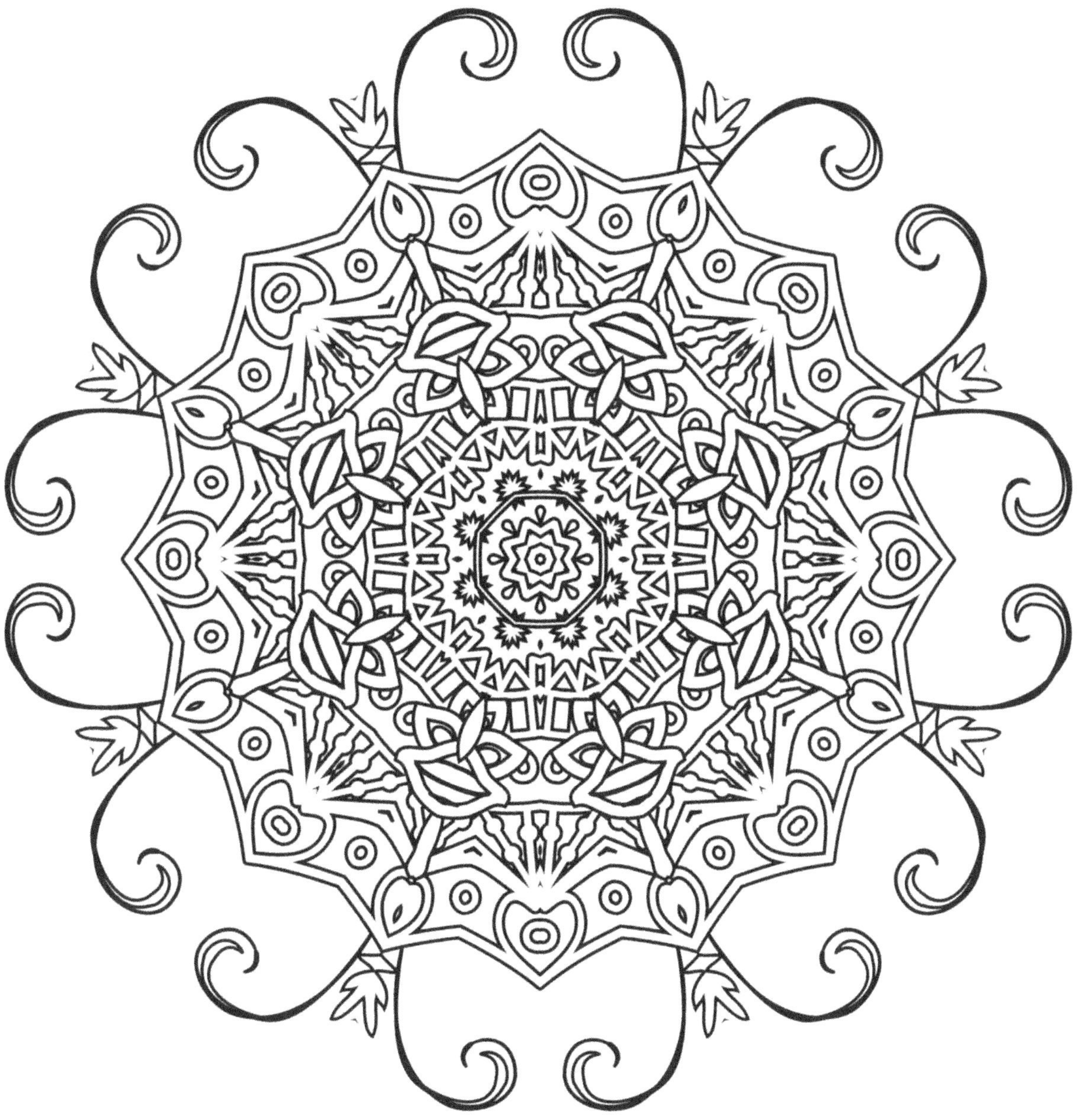

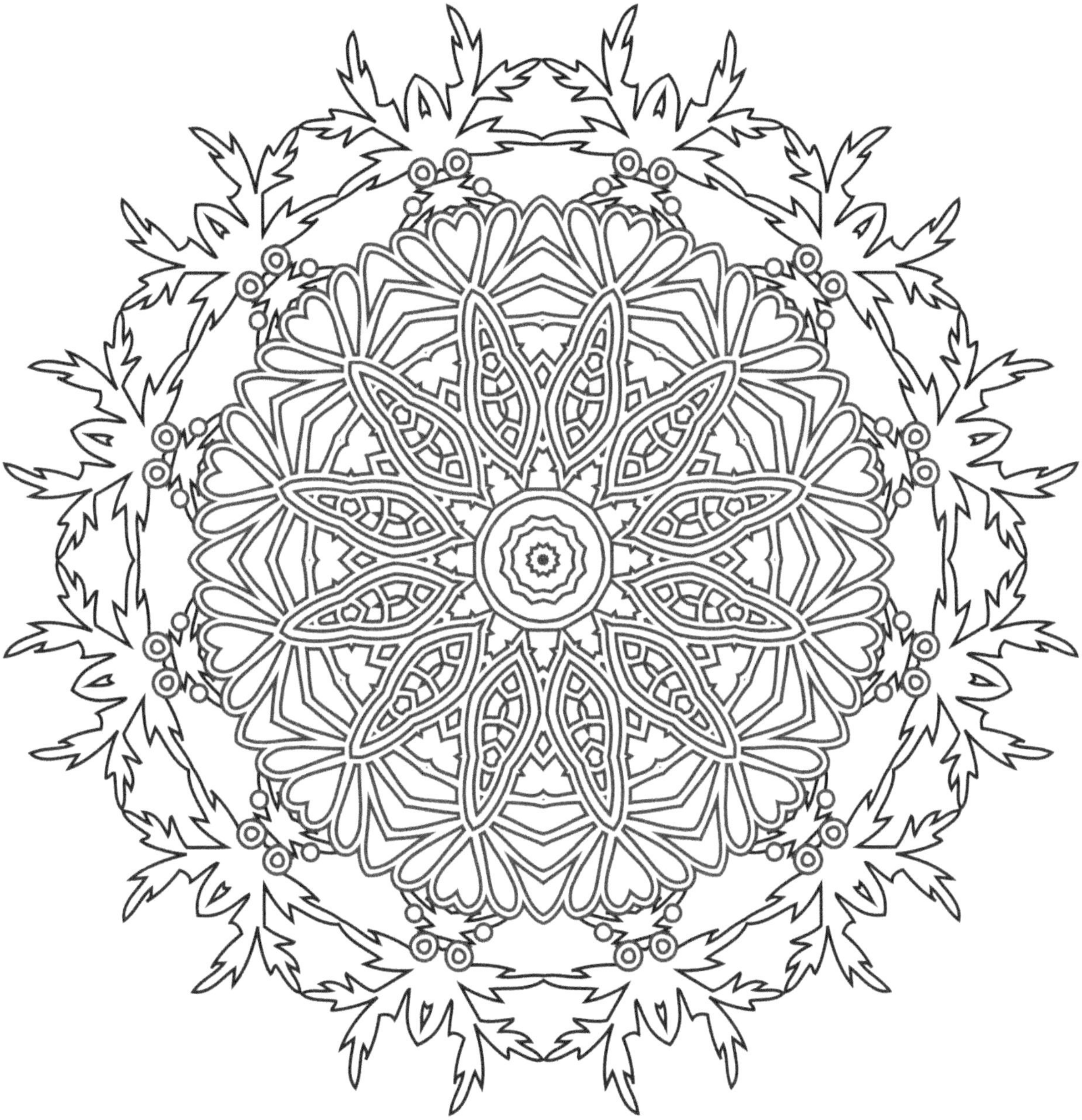

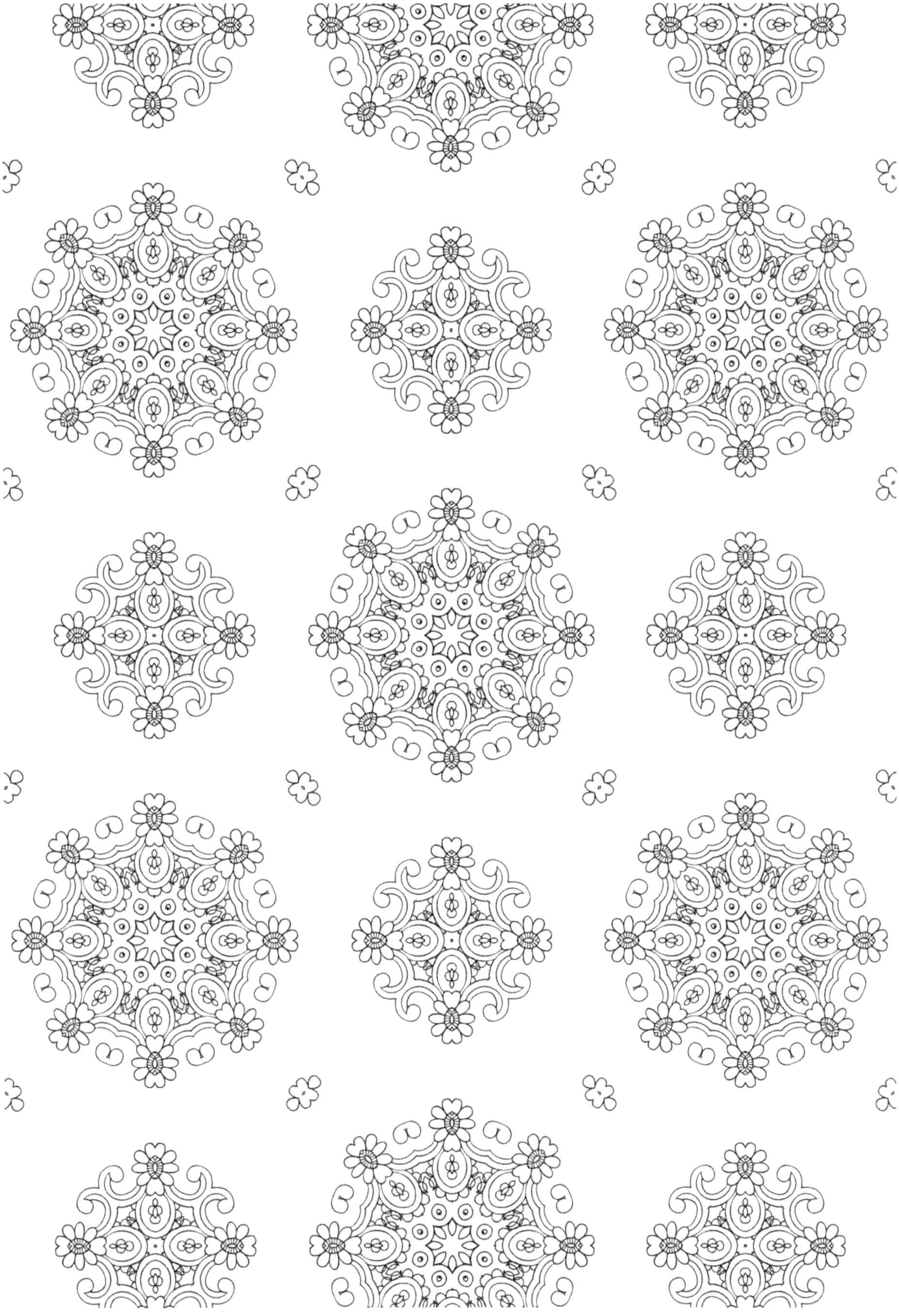

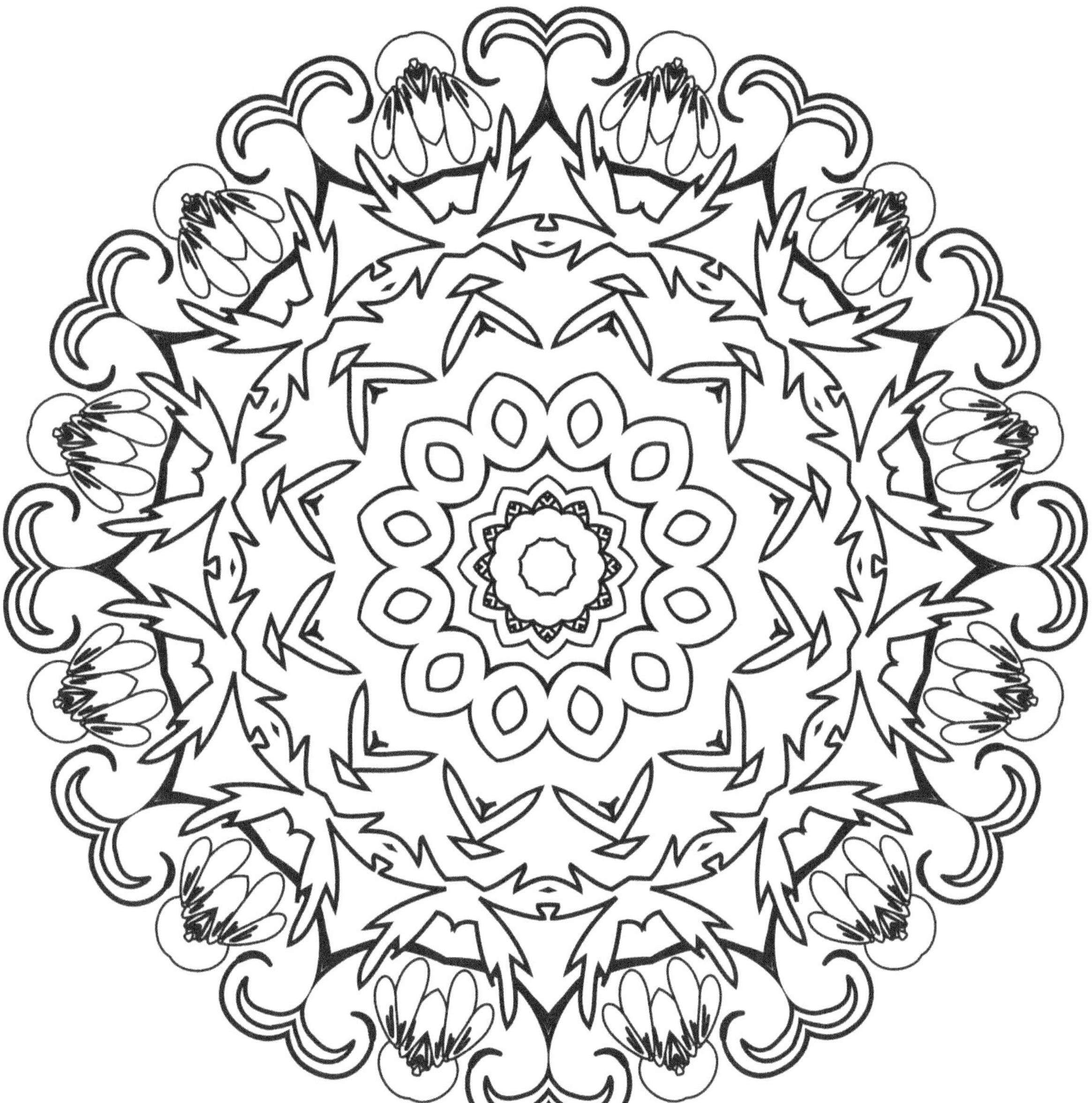

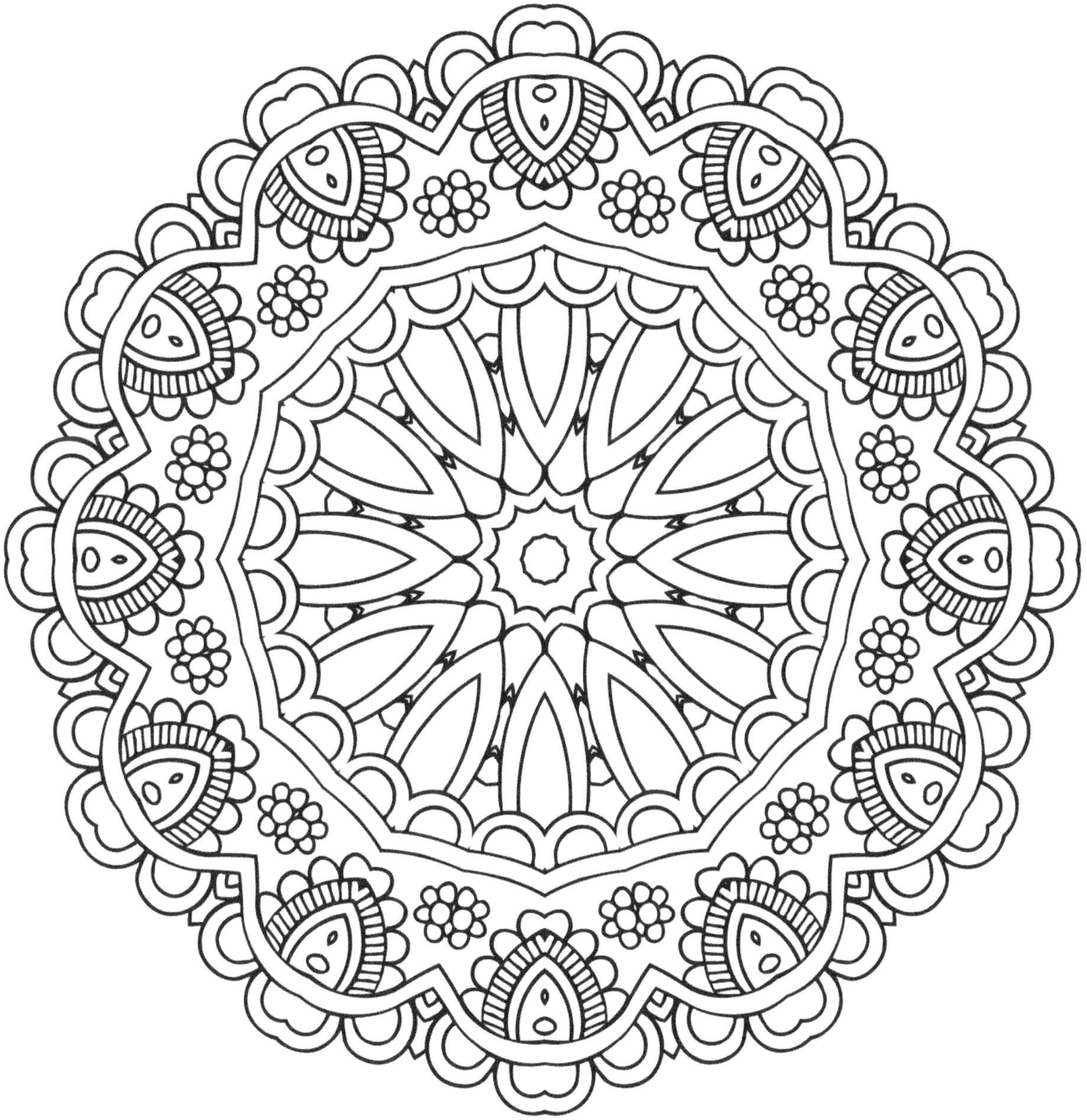

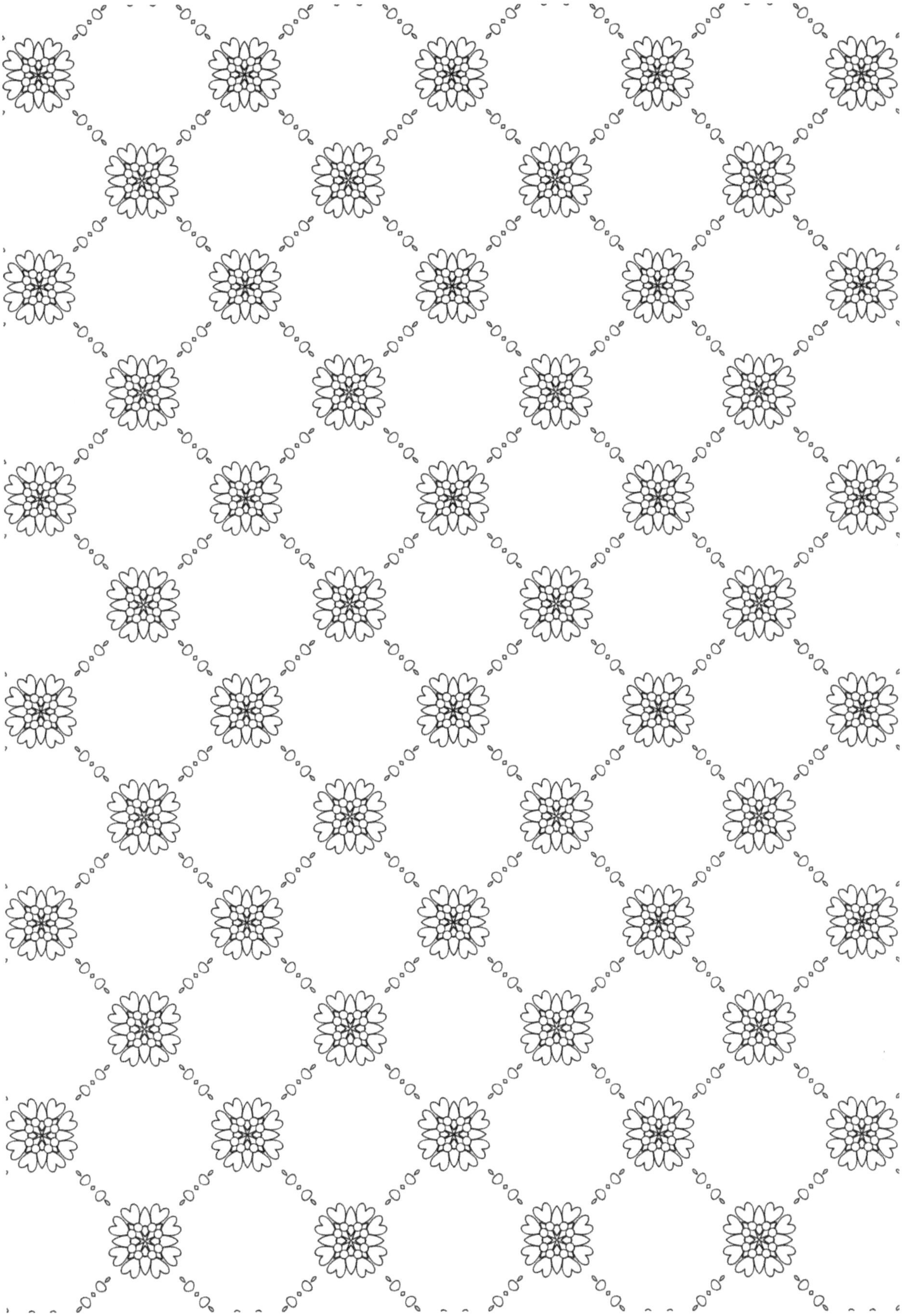

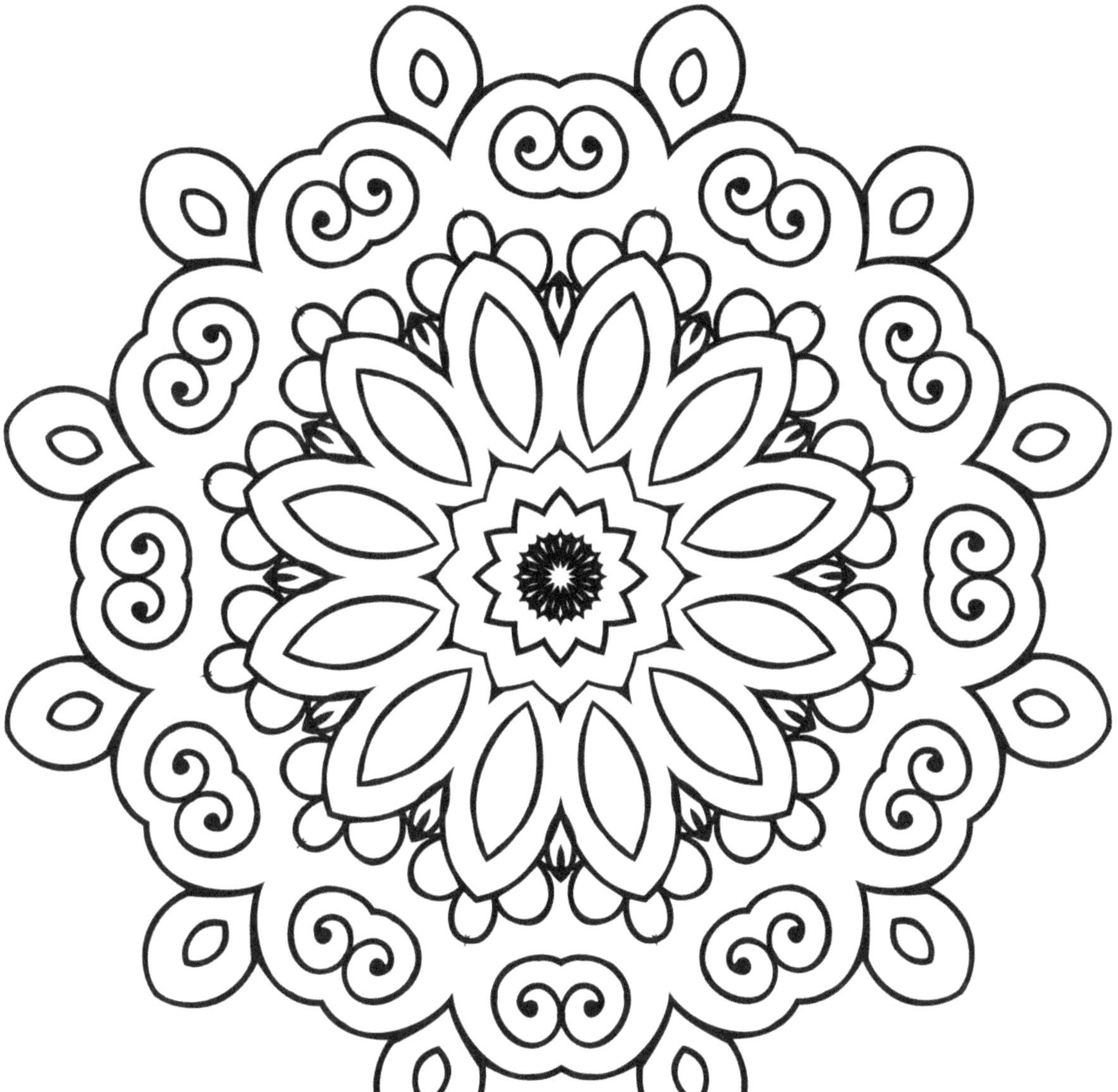

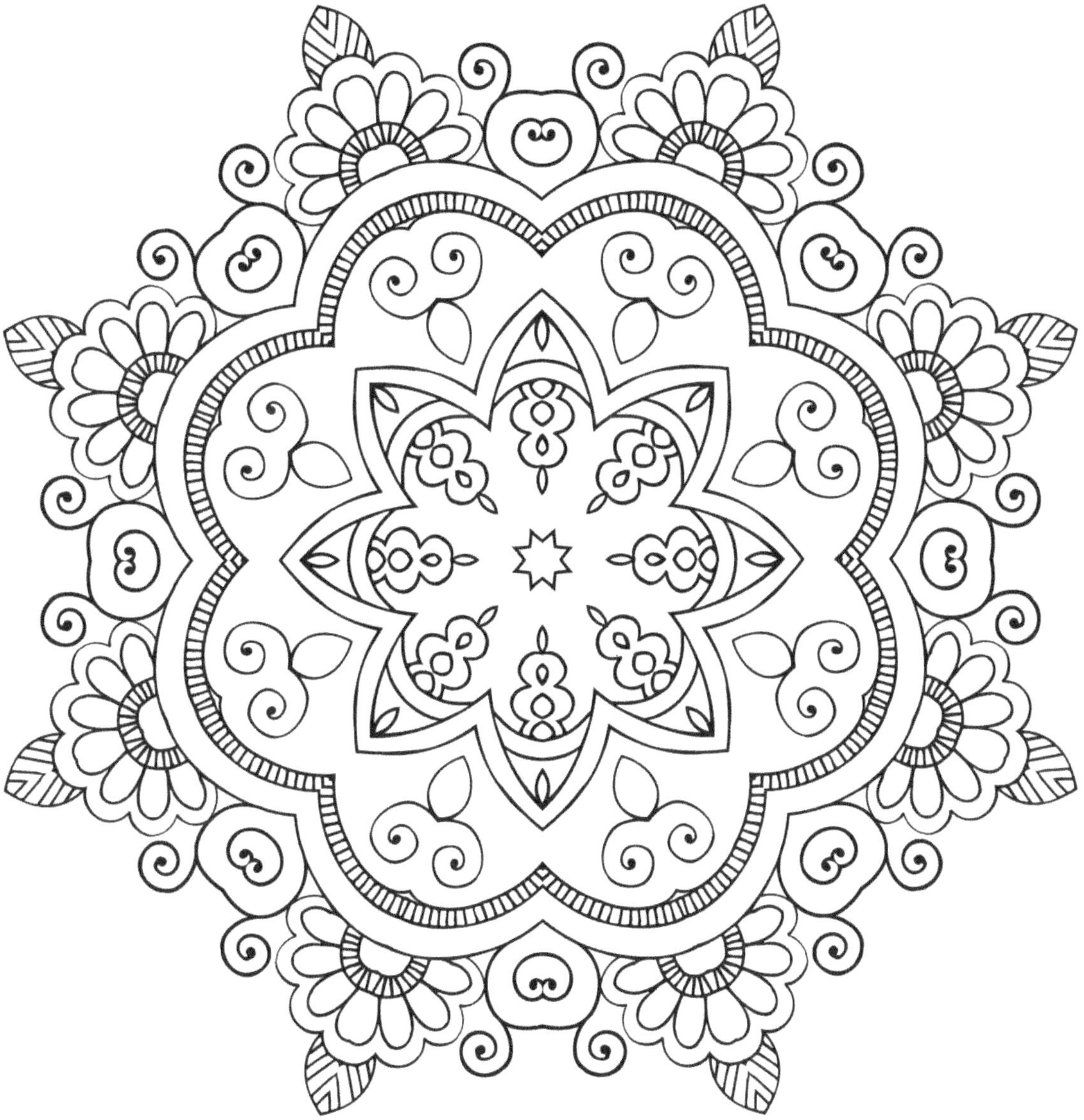

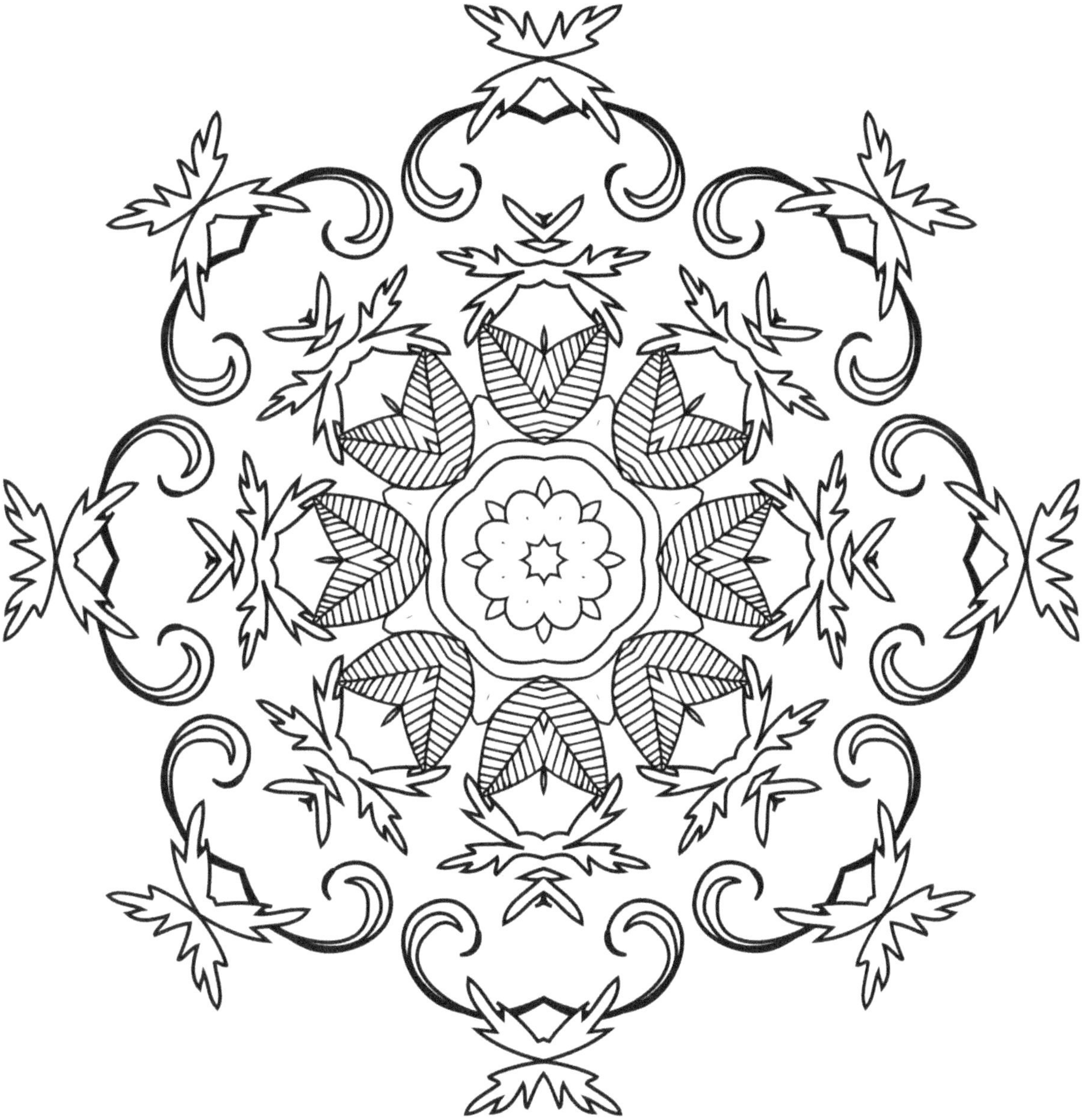

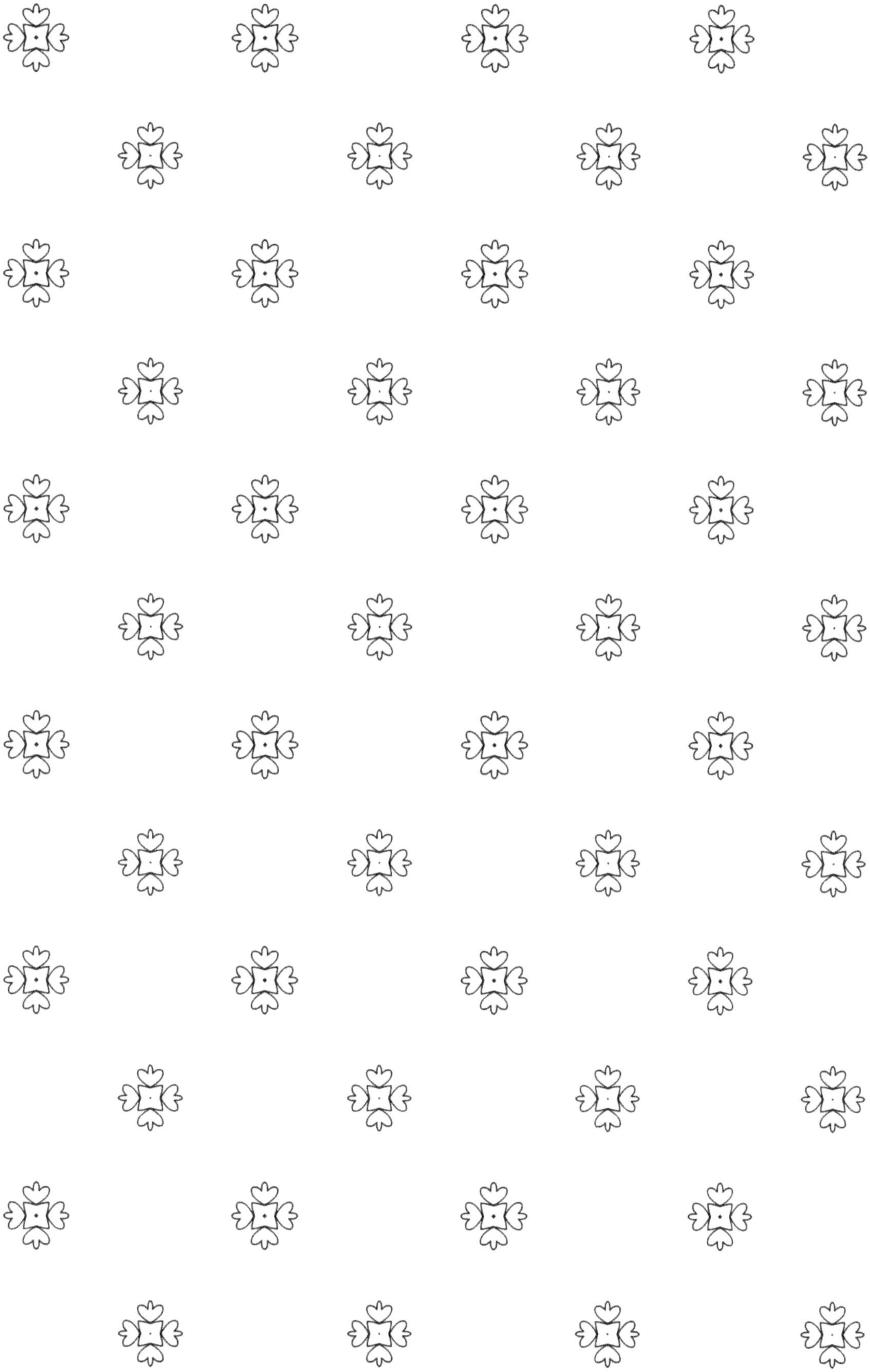

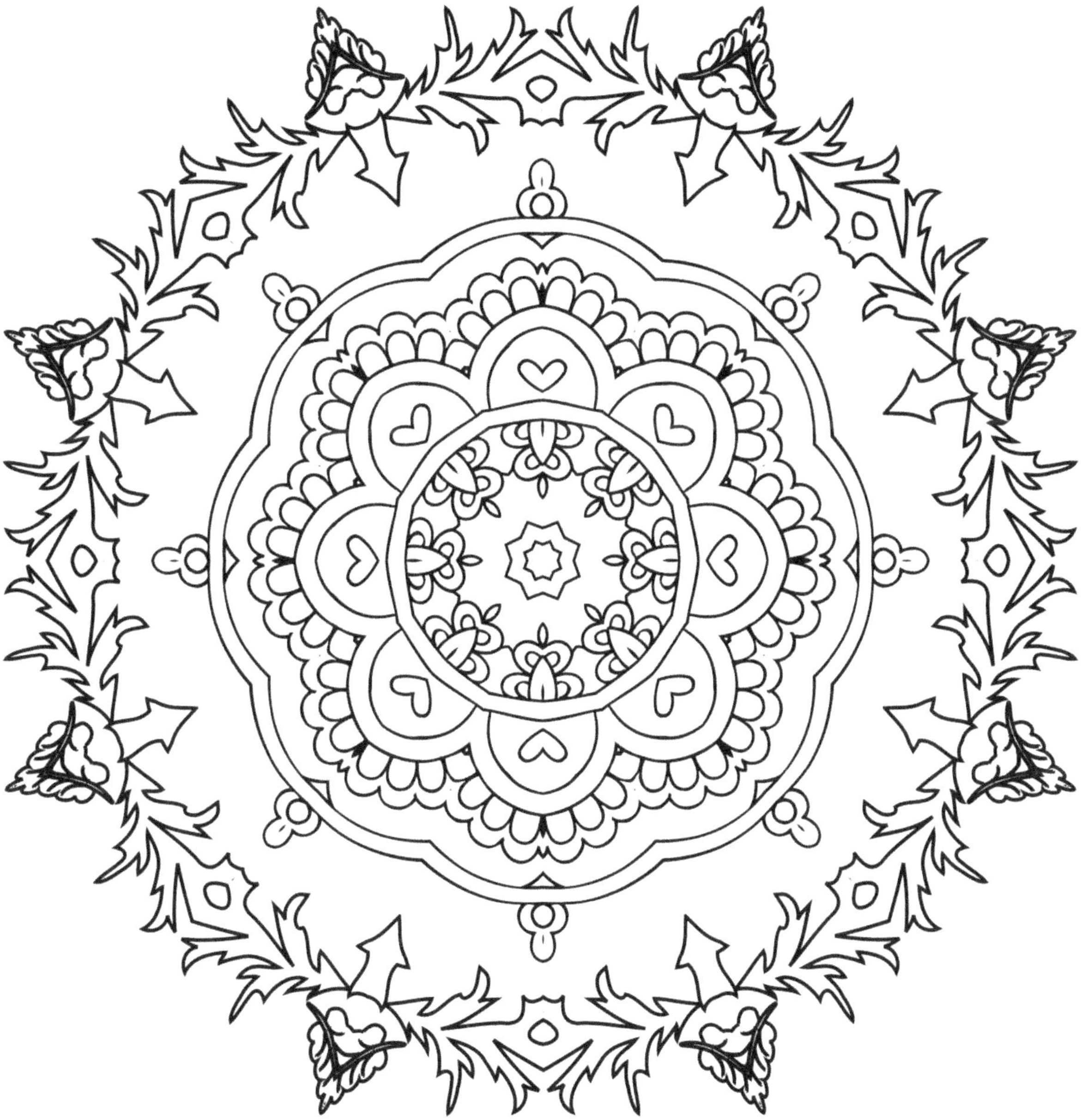

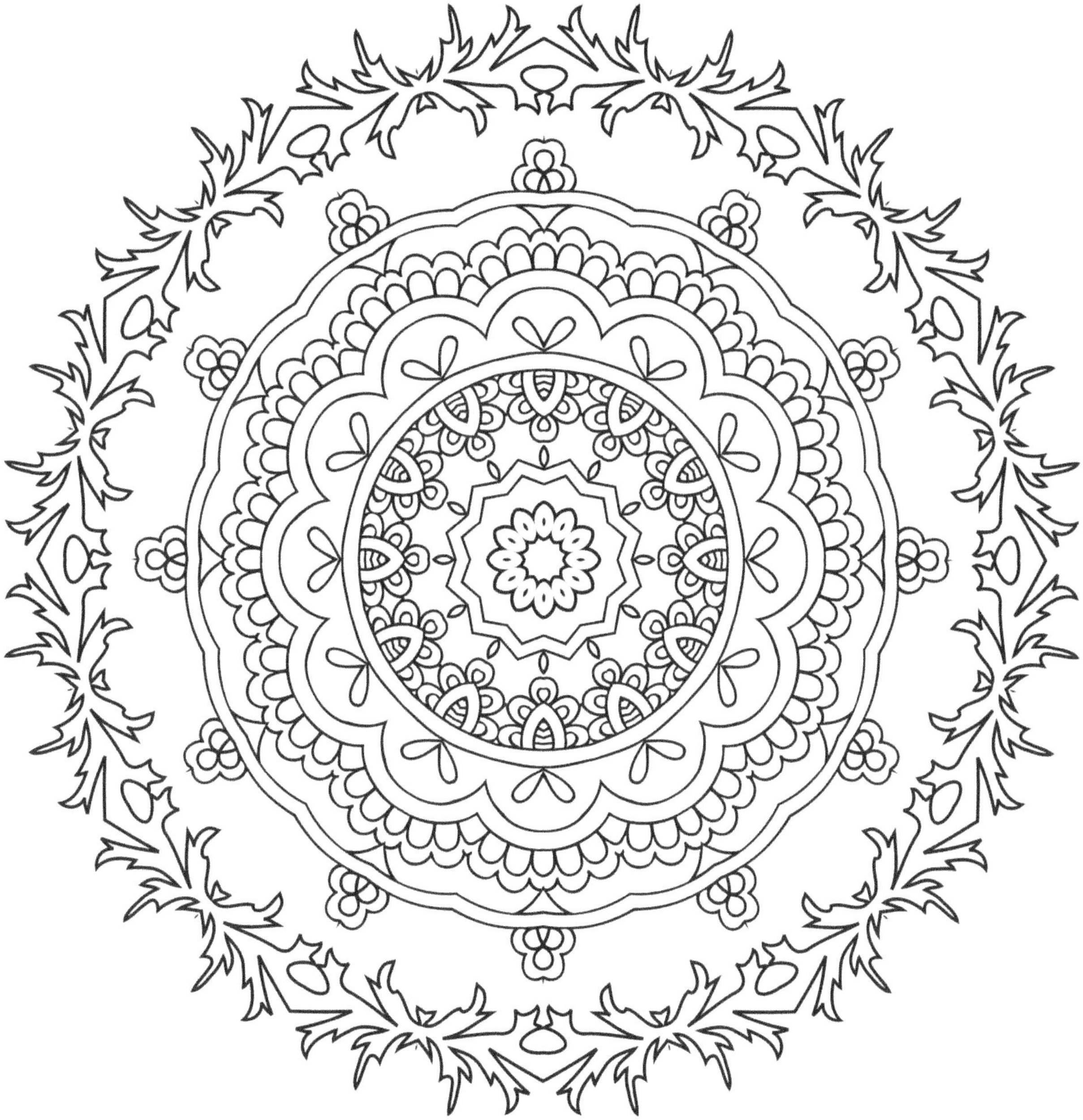

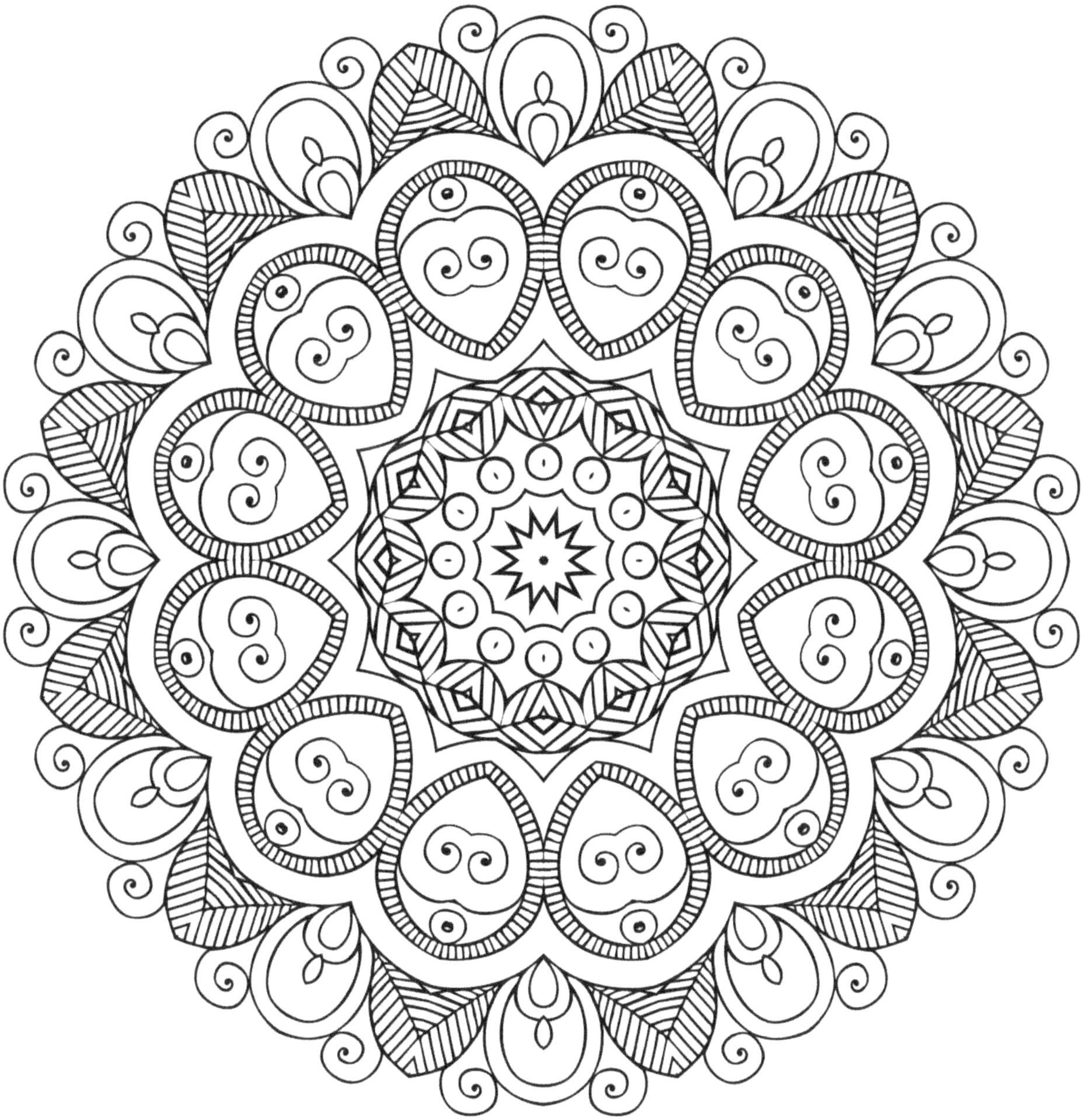

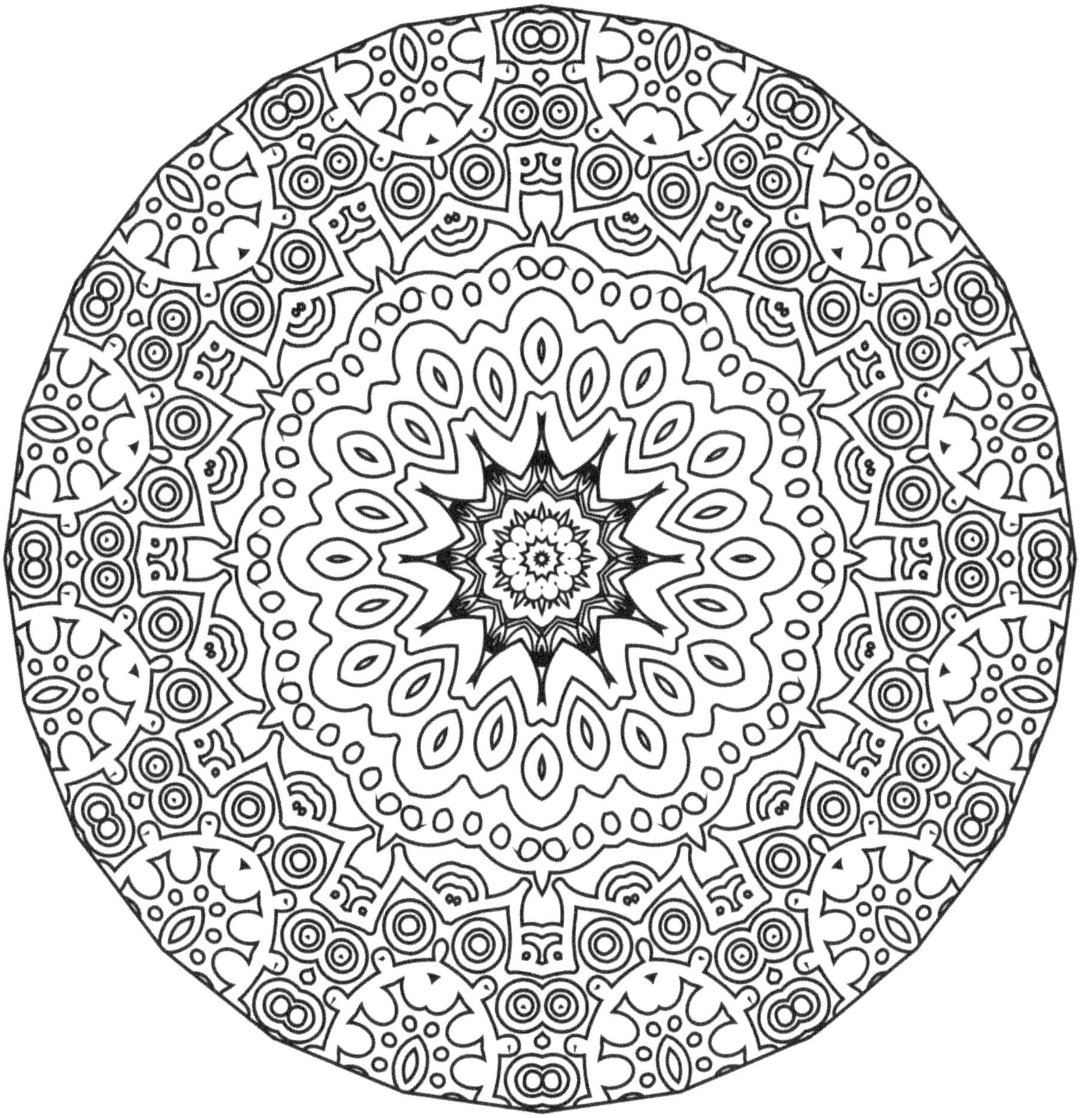

www.ingramcontent.com/pod-product-compliance
Lightning Source LLC
Chambersburg PA
CBHW080545190526
45169CB00007B/2645
9781537552279